THE ULSTER PEOPLE

IAN ADAMSON

THE ULSTER PEOPLE

Ancient, Medieval and Modern

First published by **Pretani Press**, 1991

78 ABBEY STREET, BANGOR, BT20 4JB

A Nosmada Book

Typeset by Island Publications, Belfast

Printed in Northern Ireland by The Universities Press, Belfast

Paperback   ISBN   0 948868 13 9
Hardback   ISBN   0 948868 14 7

For Violet,
With Love

Acknowledgements

The author is thankful to Professor Ronald Buchanan of the Institute of Irish Studies, Queen's University of Belfast, Michael Hall and Ian Sinclair for constructive suggestions in the preparation of the manuscript.   He fully appreciates all the help given by family, friends and scholars alike although their opinions are not necessarily those held by the author. Special thanks are due to Anne Johnston and Alison Hogg for the cartography and to Vera Govan for her care and patience in typing and retyping the manuscript.

Contents

Preface

When I first began to write books on Ulster history in the late 1960s it was in an attempt to fill the obvious vacuum which existed in general public awareness concerning the real roots of the people of Northern Ireland. The increasing violence and depressing communal tragedy which has continued over the past two decades has only highlighted the need to make available to Ulster's divided community some very pertinent facts about their unseen, but very real, shared history and heritage.

Little did I realise then that my own work would itself become part of the debate, gaining acceptance from all sections of the community, but at the same time coming under attack from those whose stereotyped views of Irish history were seriously disturbed by what was being revealed. However, some of the more critical comments came from the most unexpected of quarters — the academic establishment — though time has since taught me much about the possible motives at work within that arena, and I can now readily sympathise with Burnett Bolloten, whose highly revealing book on the 1936 Spanish Revolution, *The Grand Camouflage*, was, according to Vernon Richards, "sabotaged by the academics who monopolise the Reviews and who resented the intrusion of a mere journalist in a subject that they had just 'discovered' as a lucrative field of exploitation, as well as the fact that Bolloten undermined the whole basis of their elitist approach..."

One of the main claims made against me was that I was "indulging in pure revisionism". 'Revisionism', as the word implies, means to 'revise' one's interpretation of history, though often the word is also used in a pejorative sense, implying that the revision is deliberately undertaken to help substantiate the revisionist's own particular 'slant' on our past.

When *The Cruthin* was written, some twenty years ago, such a charge of revisionism might have seemed to contain some validity. After all, terms and concepts such as 'the Cruthin people', 'the non-Celtic Irish', 'the Galloway connection', etc — appeared at that time to be confined mostly to my own work. Indeed, Michael Hall's summation of my writings in *Ulster—the Hidden History* must have seemed so unfamiliar to the reviewer in the *Linen Hall Review*, that the latter concluded that the historical thesis being expounded aimed "at nothing less than an overthrow of current perceptions".

To introduce something apparently so 'new' into the historical debate might, therefore, have served to confirm the 'revisionist' label. Yet before we come to such a conclusion, let us consider the following quotes:

> In the north [of Ireland] the people were Cruithni, or Picts... If the [Uí Néill] failed to subdue the south thoroughly, they succeeded in crushing the Ultonians, and driving them ultimately into the south-eastern corner of the province. They plundered and burned Emain Macha, the ancient

seat of the kings of the Ultonians, and made "sword land" of a large part of the kingdom... Consequent on the [Uí Néill] invasion of Ulster [was] an emigration of Irish Cruithni or Picts [to Scotland]... The men of the present Galloway were part of the tribe known in Ireland as Cruithni, that is Picts, and only differed from the Picts of [Scotland], in having come into Galloway from Ireland.

To readers aware of the present controversy these quotes might appear to be a reasonable précis of some of my own writings. In fact, I am not the author of the quotes: they have been taken from the ninth edition of the *Encyclopaedia Britannica*, published between 1876 and 1886 — over a hundred years ago! The *Britannica*'s historical interpretation was not an isolated one, however — many books of the period took a similar approach. In 1919 the eminent Irish Nationalist historian Eoin MacNeill wrote: "When Ireland emerges into the full light of written history, we find the Picts a very powerful people in east Ulster... In Ulster, the ruling or dominant population of a large belt of territory, extending from Carlingford Lough to the mouth of the Bann, is named in the Annals both by the Latin name Picti, and its Irish equivalent Cruithni. They continue to be so named until the eighth century, when apparently their Pictish identity ceased to find favour among themselves." Bishop McCarthy, in his edition of Adamnan's *Life of St Columba* wrote that "no fact in the pagan history of Ireland is more certain than that the whole country was originally held by the Irish Picts."

Contemporary thinking in Northern Ireland was summed up by H C Lawlor, who wrote in a publication for the Belfast Natural History and Philosophical Society in 1925:

In those early times, when the history of Ireland begins to emerge from absolute obscurity or mythology, we find the country divided into five distinct Kingdoms, of which the Northern was known as Coiced Uloth or Cuigeadh Uladh, meaning the Firth of the Uluti. This district was larger than the nine counties now called Ulster, and the indigenous inhabitants appear to have been a race variously called the Qreteni or Cruithni, but more familiarly known as the Irish Picts.

About the fourth century BC or earlier, a new race appears to have come to Ireland, commonly known as the Celts or Gaels; whence they came is uncertain. From ancient mythology and other sources it appears that they were a race of yellow-haired big-bodied people, contrasting in these respects with the aborigines. They came as conquerors; they appear to have landed in Ireland on the south-east coast, gradually pushing their way north and west, eventually establishing their chief and central head-quarters at Tara in County Meath. That they drove the aborigines before them as one would drive herds of sheep is inconceivable; they conquered them and became the ruling class, holding the natives under them as serfs; they were apparently a small minority of the population.

In 1932 the Minister for Industry and Commerce of the Irish Free State (Saorstát Eireann) commissioned an *Official Handbook* in which Eoin MacNeill wrote:

> While the Celts were still newcomers to Ireland and Britain, the inhabitants of both countries were known to them by the name Pretani or Qreteni. From Qreteni came their old name in Irish—Cruithin. The old Celtic name for Ireland was Everio, for Britain, Albio. In Irish, Everio became Eriu, and afterwards Eire; Albio became Albu, then Alba. The Greeks, who knew about these islands mainly through intercourse with the Gallic Celts, called Ireland Ierne, and Britain Albion; and they called the two island the Pretanic Islands, the islands of the Pretani. The forms and application of these names were changed by Latin writers, following the example of Julius Caesar. Caesar substituted Brittani for Pretani, and gave the name to the people of Britain only, calling that island Brittania instead of Albion. Ireland was re-named Hibernia, its people Hiberni. Later on, before AD 300, a new name Scotti, began to be used in Latin for the people of Ireland, and a new name, Picti, for the people formerly called Pretani, then inhabiting the northern parts of Britain. The name Brittanic Islands was substituted for Pretanic Islands, which properly signifies the islands of the Picts.
>
> Irish traditions amply confirm the evidence of Greek writers that Ireland was once a country of the Pretani, Cruithin, or Picts. Our own writers, in the seventh century and later, show that in their time there were numerous families, including many of high degree, in every quarter of Ireland but especially in Ulster and Connacht, who were recognised to be of Pictish descent. The problem 'Who were the Picts?' has long been under discussion. Ancient and firm tradition, in Britain as well as in Ireland, declared them to be quite a distinct people from the Gaels and the Britons; and some who have sought to solve the problem have ignored the existence of a large Pictish element in Ireland. The view of the late Sir John Rhys appears most reasonable, that, whereas the Celts came from Mid-Europe and belonged to the 'Indo-European' linguistic group, the Picts belong to the older peoples of Western Europe They were the chief people of Ireland in the Bronze Age, and to them the Irish arts and crafts and monuments of that age may be ascribed.

While I have clarified and amended such historical interpretations, having taken into consideration more recent archaeological and historical conclusions, the direction of my enquiry is in fundamentally the same vein. Yet in the second half of this century there occurred among the academic establishment a definite change in emphasis. The Irish somehow came to be considered as most definitely Celts, and references to pre-Celtic population groups such as the Cruthin were unaccountably deleted from most history publications. Even the present (dare I say 'revised') edition of the *Britannica*, in its section on

Irish history, no longer makes mention of the Cruthin or even the 'Galloway connection'.

Indeed, when we look closely at much of the academic material brought out over this period, it would appear that extensive 'revision' *has* indeed taken place, a revision which played down these former pre-Celtic and British aspects. It is ironic, then, that if the charge of revisionism can be substantiated, it is not with relation to *The Cruthin*, but to what has been taking place since the middle of the present century among the urban élite, who have indulged in a process of selective historical awareness.

Yet, when we come to look at what has been written by a few eminent academics in the past few years, a remarkable — and for some, no doubt, uncomfortable — about-face seems to be occurring. Increasingly, historical evaluation is returning to some of that earlier thinking, with many previous misinterpretations having been corrected, of course — and it is the more-recent history that has been found 'wanting'.

For example, an inter-disciplinary gathering of scholars a few years ago acknowledged that any Celtic 'invasions' into Ireland more than probably involved population groups numerically "far inferior to the native population". Nowadays there is a growing acceptance that our predominant genetic heritage is not Celtic at all but can be traced back to the Neolithic period, with archaeologist Peter Woodman concluding: "The Irish are essentially pre-Indo-European, they are not physically Celtic." And of the pre-Celtic inhabitants of the North of Ireland, historian Francis Byrne has pointed out that, following the Uí Néill invasions into Ulster, "the bulk of the population in the reduced over-kingdom of Ulaid were the people known as Cruthin or Cruithni."

Of course, while the prominent part played by Ireland's pre-Celtic inhabitants within our historical and cultural heritage is slowly being acknowledged (or re-asserted), in some quarters such an admission is a non-starter. A well-known television presenter, appearing on the BBC (Northern Ireland) programme *The Show*, was quite adamant in his belief that the Irish were "all Celts". And one prominent local academic endeavoured to belittle the contribution the Cruthin have made to Ulster's history. Speaking on the BBC Radio programme *The Cruthin—A Common Culture?* in July, 1989, he asserted that the Cruthin "are rather minor and they're rather unimportant and they made very little influence on Irish power or politics." When we consider the contribution just one of these Cruthin made to not only Irish but European history — the abbot Comgall with his Bangor foundation — this forthright assertion is astonishingly inaccurate. And even if the Cruthin had thrown up no great historical personages such as Comgall or Congal Cláen, but had only become known to us as those ordinary people who had once formed the bulk of the Ulster population, then his assertion would still be pure elitist. For to claim that the majority of the population are "rather unimportant" indicates a strong bias against those who in real terms make up any nation's history — its own people.

It has also been said that some Loyalists have tried to use my work in their efforts to justify a sectarian position, in the hope that it might give a new credibility to the idea of a 'Protestant Ascendancy', only this time in cultural terms — a 'we were here first' mentality. How a proper reading of my work could lead to the supposition that the descendants of the Cruthin are somehow now exclusively Ulster Protestants is hard to fathom. Actually many individuals within the Protestant community are showing great interest in the *common identity* theme I have promoted for so many years and are not only feeling a new confidence in their Ulster identity, but have a desire to share this identity with the Catholic community.

Sectarian use of culture and history has never been one-sided, of course. Republicans and Nationalists have long been experts at this, only it has been accomplished with much more subtlety, is therefore less visible and has raised less comment. At times, however, Republican use of culture as a political weapon *is* explicit; as the Sinn Fein discussion booklet *Learning Irish* states: "Now every phrase you learn is a bullet in a freedom struggle. Make no mistake about it, either you speak Irish or you speak English. Every minute you are speaking English you are contributing to the sum total of English culture/language in this island. There is no in between." This 'Irish' language is supposed to be the heritage of *all* our people, yet when a group of young Nationalists were recently informed that over two dozen working-class Protestants had put their names down for a proposed class in Gaelic, they became most annoyed. Rather than being pleased to hear that the Protestant community was at last awakening to its 'true' heritage, their feeling was: "how dare *they* try to steal *our* language!"

Yet at the same time, many individuals from the nationalist community have readily admitted that the whole idea of a common identity has not only given them hope for the future, but has contributed more positively to their own historical appreciation than the dead weight of outdated and retrogressive Republican Nationalist ideology ever could.

Ironically, while protagonists in Northern Ireland still continue to argue over *past* history, their cultural heritage is even now being absorbed and enriched by new citizens coming from abroad, the latest coming from the West Indies, Africa, the Indian subcontinent and South-East Asia. Reinforcement of our identity has also come from the large Ulster communities in the USA, Canada, Australia, New Zealand and Africa.

In many ways a cultural battle is now on, in which interpretations of history are right to the forefront. It is a battle in which narrow and exclusive interpretations, which served to consolidate each community's supposed hegemony of righteousness, are under attack from a much broader and inclusive interpretation of *all* the facets which go to make up our identity. A positive outcome of this battle might just help to drag the Ulster people away from their obsessions with distorted history and the divisive attitudes of the past.

In their broadest sense the Middle Ages are described as being the period from the end of classical antiquity (or the deposition of the last W Roman emperor in 476 AD) to the Italian Renaissance (or the fall of Constantinople in 1453). These dates are approximate to two watershed dates in Ulster history — 432 AD and 1381 AD — and it is therefore within this period in Irish history that I have set the Medieval period.

Ancient

6500 BC — 432 AD

1 — An Ancient Heritage

The First   We have no evidence of human habitation in Ireland before the
Irishmen   retreat of the ice-sheets which covered almost the whole of the
island until the end of the Ice Age. The first settlers arrived
around 6,500 BC in the period known as the Mesolithic or Middle Stone Age.
They probably came from the western shores of Britain, the archaeological
evidence tending to suggest either from Galloway in south-west Scotland or
Cumbria in northern England.[1] These flint-users were hunters, fishermen and
food-gatherers who lived predominantly along the coast or in river valleys
such as the Bann. In the period after 4000 BC, during the Neolithic or Late
Stone Age, farming was introduced. Crops were grown, animals kept, and
many new types of implement were introduced. For the first time man began
to leave his mark on the thickly wooded Irish countryside.

The tombs and monuments made by these Neolithic farmers are called
'megalithic' (i.e. made of large stones), such as the *court cairns* and *dolmens*.
Ireland is extremely rich in such antiquities, with over 1,200 stone monuments
surviving today. The court cairns, which are mainly located in the north of the
island, are also found in south-west Scotland, and Séan O Ríordáin commented:
"The tombs and the finds from them form a continuous province joined rather
than divided by the narrow waters of the North Channel."[2] This connection
with Scotland is evidence of the ancient link which has existed throughout
history between what W.C. Mackenzie described as "two great and intimately
associated peoples".[3]

Megalithic   Some of the largest and most impressive monuments made by
Grandeur   the Neolithic Irish are located in the Boyne valley, the best-
known example being the great passage tomb at Newgrange, of
which Michael Herity wrote: "Newgrange is the most famous of a group of
over 300 passage graves built in cemeteries throughout Ireland [which] are
monuments to the most capable organisers, architects and artists ever to have
entered and influenced Ireland in the whole of prehistory."[4] New techniques
in dating have suggested that Newgrange could have been built around 3350
BC, making it one of the earliest stone buildings in the world.[5] The legacy of
Ireland's megalithic builders is of fundamental relevance to us today, for, as
Fleure pointed out, "The megaliths are not a matter of a vanished people and a
forgotten civilisation; they belong to the core of our heritage as western
Europeans."[6] P.A.O. Síocháin also wrote: "No longer can we look on these as
cold stones from a long dead era. Warm hands once held and gave them
meaning and purpose; touch them and you touch your past."[7]

Of the Neolithic period Peter Woodman wrote: "This part of Ireland's
prehistory lasted nearly two thousand years and in that period some remarkable

3

changes took place, changes which probably do more than any others to create the Ireland which enters history several thousand years later."[8] The legacy of these early settlers of Ireland is very much *our* heritage, for, despite the seemingly great distance in time which separates us from them, we are in reality just the latest generations to have sprung from a very ancient people. As archaeologist Peter Harbinson commented: "We can say in all probability that [they] represent the basic human stock onto whose blood-gene pool all subsequent peoples were 'grafted', so they may truly be described as the first Irish men and women, the ancestors of the Irish people of today."[9]

The Elder Faiths   Just as these first peoples were our distant ancestors, and we must therefore share many of their *physical* attributes — amended of course by the various invading minorities who turned their attention to Ireland in later historical periods — so also is it quite conceivable that we have retained some residue of the *personalities* of these early peoples, particularly in our relationship to the land and the seasons, a matter of life-giving importance to an agricultural community. Whatever beliefs they held — what we now call the Elder Faiths — have obviously long disappeared, yet perhaps it is possible to detect faint echoes of them in long-established rural superstitions and folk memories.

Estyn Evans wrote that archaeology was now tending to "confirm what recent anthropological, linguistic and ethnographic research suggests, that the roots of regional personality in north-western Europe are to be found in the cultural experience of pioneer farmers and stockmen, quickened by the absorption of Mesolithic fisherfolk... One should probably look to the primary Neolithic/megalithic culture rather than to the intervening Bronze Age as the main source of the Elder Faiths."[10] Professor John Kelleher commented: "The culture that reasserted itself in the fourteenth century and continued viable... down to the early seventeenth century was but the latest stage of the culture that had existed continuously and strongly since prehistoric times... We can be sure that much of it survives in the native population, if only below the level of consciousness."[11]

The visible reminders of Ireland's ancient inhabitants — the dolmens, stone circles and other burial monuments — are still treated with respect by country people. Tampering with these monuments can even today, according to some, bring bad luck upon the perpetrators, and archaeologists have been refused permission to excavate some monuments because of local resistance. At the beginning of the century W.G. Wood-Martin wrote: "Facts which show the resentment formerly felt by the country people at their disturbance, are well known. It is noteworthy that these former objects of the peasants' veneration were erected by an early wave of population. It may be suggested that their preservation by means of veneration for traditional beliefs points to the continued influence, up to a very late date, of their builders."[12]

Ironically, this veneration can today prove itself a useful ally to our present

4

concerns with conservation of the natural environment. In 1989 Irish documentary-maker Eamon de Buitléar filmed the wildlife which inhabited an ancient overgrown ringfort, which for hundreds of years the local population had left untouched because of their belief that the 'little people' still lurked among its bushes and trees. As a result the resident animals had flourished, with little fear of man. "Animals realise these are the places to inhabit. There are cases of council workmen refusing to make a road through an area containing a 'fairy fort' because they have certain knowledge of men elsewhere who were cursed for interfering with such places. These beliefs guarantee conservation."[13]

There has also survived in Ireland an extensive body of customs and beliefs regarding the observance of particular times, dates and festivals — centred around the practical needs of a people whose livelihood was based upon the growing of corn and the raising of cattle, in other words a farmer's calendar. Kevin Danaher has shown that this 'folk calendar' was not Celtic, and suggests: "We may conclude that the four-season calendar of modern Irish tradition is of very high antiquity, even of late neolithic or megalithic origin, and that its beginnings predate the early Celts in Ireland by at least as great a depth of time as that which separates those early Celts from us."[14]

Regional   Estyn Evans summarised the importance of this long period of
Diversity   habitation and consolidation, remarking also upon the evidence
of a regional diversity: "The [archaeological] evidence... reveals one essential truth: that we are dealing not with mythical 'lost tribes' but with ancestral West Europeans, physically our kinsmen, who were the first Ulster farmers, pioneering in a way of life which has persisted through more than 5000 years, carrying with it attitudes of reverence for the forces of nature and leaving indelible marks on the face of the land. The landscape they helped to fashion was to be the heritage — for good or ill — of all later settlers, Celt and Christian, Norman and Planter. Already by the late Neolithic, farmers practising shifting cultivation and rearing livestock had penetrated all the major upland areas in the province and had reduced considerable stretches of forest to grassland, scrub or bog. During the early Bronze Age it seems likely that 'much of the remaining forest was destroyed or degraded' by cultivators and stock-raisers who had learnt to use metal axes and whose favourite cereal was barley, a crop which has become dominant once more in recent years. No doubt many forests remained in the ill-drained lowlands, but we must not assume that they were entirely virgin. Rivers and lakes among the forests would have harboured mesolithic remnants, and the damp lowlands would anyhow have acted as divides, so that different cultural areas can be discerned. Repeatedly, Antrim and North Down — the prehistoric core-area — stand out in Bronze Age distribution maps as a distinctive region, supporting a vigorous metal industry and a far-reaching export trade despite poor mineral resources."[16]

Bronze Age   The introduction of metallurgy into Ireland is generally ascribed to those artisans who also made a type of pottery to which the name Beaker has been given. Three objects found near Conlig, County Down, include a copper knife or dagger of Beaker type, a small copper axe of early type and a small copper dagger of more advanced type. The mines of Conlig are still extant and the area was probably the main source of copper ore in the north.

The working of bronze commenced in Ireland around 1800 BC. In the beginning the ancient Irish bronzesmiths provided the needs of much of Britain, and to a lesser extent of northern and western Europe as well. That such a great bronze industry should be carried out on an island where tin, which accounts for some 10 per cent of the alloy, was not mined to any degree, indicates that this component must have come from Cornwall, Brittany or even North Spain. It was once thought that the new pottery styles and burial practices adopted at this time indicated large immigrations into Ireland, but more weight is now given to indigenous development, with 'influences' rather than 'invasions' coming in from abroad.

Ireland's   About 1200 BC there was a change in the type of artefacts
Golden Age   produced and a whole new variety appears, distinctive of what we know as the Late Bronze Age: there were torques of twisted gold, gorgets of sheet gold, and loops of gold with expanded ends used as dress fasteners. This was indeed a Golden Age for Ireland, peaceful and prosperous, controlled by a society in which craftsmen were even more in evidence than warriors, and open to trading influences from abroad. Irish artefacts have been discovered not only in nearby France and Scandinavia but as far afield as Poland.

The advancement of the ancient people of those times in the science of navigation has been very much underrated, and the geographer E.G. Bowen has concluded that the seas around Ireland were "as bright with neolithic argonauts as the Western Pacific is today."[16] Certainly, with north-east Ireland and south-west Scotland separated, at their closest points, by only thirteen miles, and considering that much of the land was still covered with dense forest, the North Channel of the Irish Sea would have acted not as a barrier but as a more effective means of communication between these two areas.

The Prophet Ezekiel, writing about 500 BC, in his address to the people of Tyre (in ancient Phoenicia), gives an indication of such a widespread trading network: "They have made thy shipboards of fir trees of Senir, and have taken cedar trees of Lebanon to make thy masts. Of the oaks of Bashan have they made thine oars; the company of Asurites have made thine hatches of well worked ivory, brought out of Chittim. It was of fine linen and Phrygian broidered work from Egypt which thou madest thy spreading sails; and thy covering was of the blue and purple of the isles of Elishas." Could this mention of the 'rich purple dyes' be a reference to the British Isles? The purple dyes of our islands were celebrated among the later Greeks and Romans and were very expensive.

'Isles of the Pretani' Between 600 and 500 BC 'Periplous' of Himilco, the Carthaginian, made the earliest documentary reference to Ireland. The Greek philosopher Aristotle, who lived in the fourth century BC, wrote of an island called Ierne which lay at the edge of the continent, and stated that it was discovered by the Phoenicians. The sister island was known as Albion. These names had come to the general knowledge of Greek geographers such as Eratosthenes by the middle of the third century BC. Between 330 and 300 BC the Greek geographer and voyager Pytheas, in his *Concerning the ocean*, gave us the earliest reference to the British Isles, calling them the Isles of the Pretani (*Pretanikai nesoi*). The 'Pretani' are thus the most ancient inhabitants of Britain and Ireland to whom a definite name can be given. As there is no evidence of any major immigrations into Ireland after the neolithic period, the Pretani would appear to be the direct descendants of the earlier peoples, or at least a dominant segment within the native population. In the later Irish literature 'Pretani' would become 'Cruthin'.

The Celts Ireland was now to encounter a significant group of immigrants — the Celts — who were to bring with them a new and rich language. We cannot be certain as to when the first groups of Celtic people arrived in Ireland. To this day, there is no evidence which can place Celtic settlements in Ireland before the first century AD or the first century BC at the earliest. The once-popular notion that the Celts were in Ireland from time immemorial has long been discarded. Another popular belief, however, that the Celtic immigrants, when they did arrive, swamped the local inhabitants and became the majority population, has proven harder to dislodge. Yet it is now generally accepted that when those groups of peoples we loosely call 'Celts' arrived in Ireland, they did so in small numbers. A seminar held by the Irish Association of Professional Archaeologists in 1984 acknowledged that any Celtic 'invasions' were more than probably carried out by numbers "far inferior to the native population(s)".[17] Archaeologist Peter Woodman has also pointed out: "The gene pool of the Irish was probably set by the end of the Stone Age when there were very substantial numbers of people present and the landscape had already been frequently altered. The Irish are essentially Pre-Indo-European, they are not physically Celtic. No invasion since could have been sufficiently large to alter that fact completely."[8]

Popular notions, particularly when they are interwoven with cultural pride and romantic ideas of a nation's ethnic identity, make it difficult at times to permit new awareness from percolating into public consciousness. While this is forgivable for the general public, it is harder to understand why some academics and media presenters still talk today of the Irish as being a 'pure' Celtic people, despite all the mounting evidence to the contrary.

Although they had come as a minority, the Celts eventually achieved a dominant position in those areas that came under their sway, and they formed a warrior aristocracy, wielding power over the mass of indigenous inhabitants.

Celtic origins   The word 'Celtic' is primarily a linguistic term which is applied to a closely related group of dialects referred to as 'Indo-European'. There is little doubt that the Celtic tribes of Europe were composed of different physical types, and that Celtic speech was adopted by or imposed upon large numbers of subjects. The Celts became dominant over most of Central Europe, and various groups of Celtic peoples migrated from there to other parts of the continent.

When the Roman empire expanded, her legions came into direct confrontation with this Celtic heartland, and Caesar's famous 'Gallic Wars' (58-51 BC) not only gives us a personal account of Gaul (modern-day France, Belgium, northern Italy and part of Germany) but of how the Romans extinguished its independence. It was quite possibly in response to Roman expansion that some Celtic groups crossed from continental Europe to the British Isles.

Yet the Roman destruction of Celtic power had been preceded by another, far more fundamental encounter. The intrusion of the Celts themselves into Europe must have been, as Professor Thomas Markey noted, "one of the most wrenching cultural collisions of all time, the clash between Indo-Europeans and non-Indo-Europeans in early Western Europe." [18]

What of the pre-Celtic inhabitants of Ireland? Markey pointed out that "Ireland was the final stronghold of the Megalithic peoples in the West, and the Celts who subsequently settled there were the last Indo-Europeans to come into contact with them." These pre-Celtic people obviously didn't disappear, but survived, and remained as the majority population. As Francis Byrne noted: "The earlier, non-Indo-European, population, of course, survived under the Celtic overlordship. One group in particular, known to the P-Celts as *Pritani* and to the Irish as *Cruithni*, survived into historical times as the Picts or 'painted people' of Scotland. The Cruithni were numerous in Ulster too, and the Loíges of Leinster and possibly the Ciarraige of Connacht and north Kerry belonged to the same people." [19]

The 'forgotten'   Although it is now clear that the Celts were relative
Irishmen   latecomers to Ireland, and that when they arrived here they
most probably did so in small numbers, their presence has been accorded a remarkable prominence, not the least because of their introduction of a new language. The 1984 seminar held by the Irish Association of Professional Archaeologists, attended not only by archaeologists but representatives from linguistics and environmental studies, deliberated on the theme 'The origins of the Irish', and the moderator of the seminar pointed out: "An Irishman was defined as one who spoke either the earliest form of the Irish language or a language immediately ancestral to it. Such a definition then

pertains to the appearance of Irish-speaking Celts and is not... to be confused with the arrival of the first people in Ireland." [17] Thus the earlier, majority population of Ireland, who had inhabited the island for a greater length of time than that which separates the Celts from us today, were denied the epithet 'Irish' in favour of the Celts. The 'earliest form of the Irish language' referred to was not, as one might reasonably suppose, that spoken by the original inhabitants, but the specific language, now known as Gaelic, introduced by an incoming Celtic minority.

As far back as 1906 Eoin McNeill, founder of the Gaelic League and one of the most eminent of Irish historians, believed that his research had finally penetrated through the academic obsession with the Celts to allow us to acknowledge the vital part played in our heritage by the original inhabitants. He wrote that "the hitherto current account of pre-Christian Ireland has belittled and overclouded the vast majority of the Irish people for the glorification of a dominant minority," and he felt he could now safely assert that "the one outcome of [these] studies has been to restore the majority to the historical place of honour from which they have been ousted for a thousand years." [20] He had obviously spoken too soon. The Celts have certainly contributed richly to the cultural legacy of the Irish, yet they are only one aspect of a heritage which is more ancient and varied than people are generally aware.

The Irish Language Ironically, it is through the very languages introduced by Indo-European peoples such as the Celts that we are now beginning to learn more about the *pre*-Celtic peoples who were finally to adopt such languages as their own. Heinrich Wagner wrote: "It is likely that the [Celtic invasions] did not involve large numbers of Indo-European-speaking peoples, a view which has led a number of scholars, including myself, to believe that in the British Isles Indo-European language as imposed by small bands of Celtic invaders from the Continent must have been influenced strongly by the speaking habits of a predominantly non-Celtic population." [21] So Gaelic would eventually become, not a pure Celtic language, but, as David Green described it, "simply the linguistic expression of the Irish people... a language made in Ireland." [22]

The 5th and 6th centuries in particular are known to have been a period of unusually rapid development in the Gaelic language, as shown by the contrast between the general language of Ogham inscriptions and the earliest Old Gaelic known from manuscripts. There is little doubt that this was due to the widespread adoption of the Gaelic speech by the original inhabitants and the passage of older words and grammatical forms into Gaelic. By this time, therefore, Gaelic had become, according to Heinrich Wagner, "one of the most bizarre branches of Indo-European" since "in its syntax and general structure it has many features in common with non-Indo-European languages." [23]

Linguistic analysis is today affording us new insights into this intermingling of peoples. In studying the various branches of 'Indo-European', scholars had of necessity to define what it actually *is* — its permissible vocabulary and grammar — and thereby define what it is *not* — its impermissible vocabulary and grammar. This 'impermissible vocabulary and grammar' was obviously that borrowed from the *pre*-Indo-European inhabitants of Europe. As Thomas Markey explains: "No Indo-European language displays an acceptably Indo-European word for 'apple', a fruit that was an invaluable part of a primitive diet. The apple was presumably unknown to Indo-Europeans in their primordial homeland, wherever that was... We may conclude that, as nomadic herdsmen, the Indo-Europeans borrowed the apple, along with terms for it, from the Megalithic farmers... We now know that something like twenty-eight percent of the Germanic lexicon, including such common words as English *folk*, have non-Indo-European origins. The language handbooks that have been accepted as the standard for decades are now badly in need of extensive revisions." [18]

This linguistic study, according to Markey, has meant that "We are now equipped with a potent filter device, a negative definer of non-Indo-European in the West [and] the silence that has long surrounded the pre-Indo-Europeans has finally been made to speak." Markey was able to identify certain fundamental differences between the two cultures. *Pre*-Indo-European society was of a matrifocal, non-stratified nature, based on a sedentary, horticultural lifestyle, where there existed advanced boat building and navigational techniques as well as a sophisticated knowledge of astronomy. Indo-European society, on the other hand, was of a patrifocal, stratified nature, with a nomadic lifestyle based on animal husbandry, and where there was a lack of boatbuilding and navigational techniques and only a rudimentary knowledge of astronomy. As Markey concludes: "Clearly, the Megalithic peoples gave more than they got. They lost their language, while the Indo-Europeans pillaged it for loans... The invader was technologically inferior to the resident." [18]

It was the discovery of iron around 800 BC which was to allow these Indo-European peoples to initiate a major technological revolution of their own, and Europe was to enter its Iron Age.

Ireland's Iron Age   The early phase of the use of iron implements in Ireland extended over about the last two centuries BC and a little beyond. It is marked by the appearance in north-east Ireland of such equipment as iron swords and their bronze scabbards whose ornamentation is based on continental rather than British models. This is consistent with the growing isolation from Britain apparent at the end of the Late Bronze Age. Implements of Late Bronze Age type continued to be a marked feature and burial customs persisted from the earlier Age. Excavations at Downpatrick showed that life continued unbroken.

None of this can be taken as evidence of a Celtic migration to Ireland, rather it shows that an ancient land of craftsmen were learning new ways. If there was a movement from the Continent it may only have been of chieftains and their retinues or of craftsmen alone. However. we may tentatively delineate this period as the beginning of Celtic influence in Ireland.

When the first groups of Celtic peoples did eventually begin to consolidate their position in various parts of Ireland, their kings took over for their royal sites the neolithic burial places still sacred to the local inhabitants. This has been partially confirmed by archaeological findings — for example, by the co-existence of Celtic Iron Age earthworks and a neolithic passage grave at the 'Mound of the Hostages' at Tara — and by Gaelic practice itself: the neolithic burial site at Knowth was chosen by the local Uí Néill kings of northern Brega as their centre from the eighth century onwards. As Francis Byrne remarked: "There can be no doubt at all of the extraordinary continuity of tradition exemplified at sites such as Tara and Knowth. This is in itself a strong argument for the survival of large elements of the megalithic people and of their beliefs in Ireland under the later Celtic overlay." [24]

More notably, it seems that the Celtic newcomers, as Estyn Evan suggested, also "reinforced an older and persistent regional distinction... Gaelic culture as a whole, like the Gaelic language, seems to have taken shape by being poured into an Irish mould, a mould having varied regional designs," and he asked, "Did the Celts conquer Ireland, or rather did Ireland conquer the Celts?" [10]

Ulster's 'Great Wall'   One of the most remarkable pieces of evidence which lends weight to the probability that regional differences pertained in Ireland in the prehistoric period, is the continued existence today of parts of a great earthwork 'wall', once topped by a wooden palisade, which can be traced from Bundoran in County Donegal to South Armagh. This 'wall', known as the Black Pig's Dyke, makes use of natural barriers and lakes for part of its length, and it must have been a formidable barrier to approaches from the south. The 'wall' is situated in a forward position within a drumlin belt, which consists of tens of thousands of "shapely streamlined mounds of boulder clay [which] provided a defence in depth for the kingdom of Ulster". [10] Aiden Walsh noted: "Firstly, the Black Pig's Dyke was not simply a two-line defence (double-bank and double-ditch); it was a three-line defence. The third line was composed of a timber palisade which paralleled the earthwork itself. Secondly, it is clear from [its] scale and nature that we are dealing with a defensive structure. The earthwork also faces south and is set on southern facing slopes to defend those on its northern side. Thirdly, it appears to have been deliberately and quite fully destroyed, presumably during wartime. The short excavation carried out in County Monaghan has told us that this stretch of the monument... was built in the last few centuries BC. Perhaps we are dealing here with... a war extending across the land starting at the boundaries of a kingdom and culminating with the destruction of its capital." [25]

At the eastern end of the 'wall' is a massive enclosure, called 'the Dorsey'. One evening in 1977, as members of an archaeological team went for an impromptu walk around the perimeter of the earthworks, they chanced upon a portion bulldozed that same day for land reclamation. To their surprise, they noticed the tops of rotted ancient posts just visible in the disturbed ground. As Chris Lynn wrote: "The discovery of this palisade underlines the strongly defensive character of the Dorsey. Its builders were not content to rely on the patch of wet bog for defence of the south-west corner but augmented the edge of the morass with the ditch and a stout palisade."[26] A dendrochronological examination was to find that the timbers used to construct the palisade around the Dorsey had been felled a few years after 100 BC.

Such massive physical constructions leave us with many unanswered questions. What of the people who were able to erect such impressive earthworks? As Victor Buckley pointed out: "The building of massive, travelling earthworks to monitor traffic northwards needed a cohesive society behind it, be it a monarchy, democracy or theocracy, which could call upon a large manpower-base and utilise vast natural resources."[27]

What of the war that has been suggested was the cause of its eventual destruction? Was this a war among the pre-Celtic peoples? Or was it between the original inhabitants and the first Celtic invaders? We will probably never know the answer, but one thing at least is certain — the history of Ireland from then on was that of a continual struggle for power between a multiplicity of factions and their ever-changing alliances.

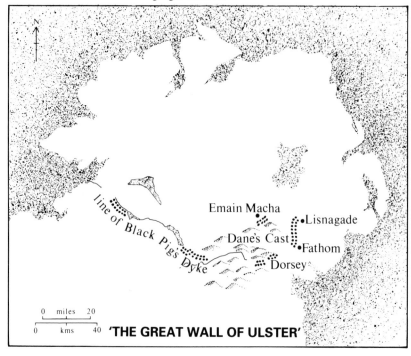

'THE GREAT WALL OF ULSTER'

2 — The Struggle for the North

Ptolemy's   In the second century AD there came from upper Egypt one of
Ireland   the greatest of ancient scientists, know to us today as Ptolemy the
Greek. He wrote a magnificent work comprising eight books, the
Geographia Hyphegesis, in which he not only gives us an account of Ireland,
but provides the earliest known map of the British Isles, on which is marked
various tribal and geographical names. At the beginning of research into
Ireland's 'Celtic' roots, the map proved disconcerting to many scholars, because
it seemed to contradict the then-assumed antiquity of the Gaelic occupation of
Ireland. The renowned Irish linguist T.F. O'Rahilly could find no evidence of
Gaelic names in Ptolemy's account and pointed out that those names which
could be traced were of Belgic British stock. To compensate it was suggested
that Ptolemy was using sources going back to the fourth century BC. Yet the
Roman occupation of the southern part of Britain had already been completed
by 84 AD, and it is difficult to believe that the great scholars of the Roman
Empire had to rely on sources 500 years old for information about an island
their soldiers could see every day from the coast of Galloway.

On Ptolemy's map is mentioned a place called *Isamnion*. Scholars now feel
that this place is the ancient capital of Ulster, called *Emain* in the earliest Irish
texts, and more generally know as Emain Macha. This ancient seat of the
kings of Ulster — still surviving today as Navan Fort — contained a great
ceremonial building, the timbers for which were felled at the same time as the
massive defensive enclosure of the Dorsey, and presumably by the same
population group.

The Arrival of   When the written records become acceptable for historical
the 'Gaels'   purposes — in the sixth and seventh centuries — the
fastest rising power in Ireland are those Celts we now call
the 'Gaels'. While this name has had to suffice as a all-embracing description
of these particular Celts, we do not know just what mixture of peoples made up
the original groups of immigrants, or in what way these newcomers soon had
other tribes grafted onto them. Indeed, in the later writings of the early
genealogists, 'Gaelic' tribes appear to gain a remarkable and posthumous
increase. The name Gael itself is derived from the Old British 'Guidel',
modern Welsh 'Gwyddel', meaning 'raider', and would suggest that the
newcomers had no common name for themselves until they had come into
contact with foreigners.

Just as we are not able to identify any particular group of Celtic invaders as
being the first 'Gaels' to arrive on Irish shores, nor can we be certain about
dates. According to Gaelic tradition itself Tuathal Techtmar had led the
ancestors of the Gaels to Ireland, where they overthrew some of the
aithechthuatha (non-Gaelic, 'unfree' peoples) and established themselves in
the area around Meath. Under the leadership of Mug Nuadat (Eogan), another

13

party of Gaels were able to establish themselves in Munster, this conquest seemingly being effected with much less conflict than that of their 'Midland' associates.

According to the genealogical material contained within 'Laud 610' the date reckoned for Tuathal's becoming king of Tara is 153 AD. Another source, Mael Mura, gave a reckoning of 135 AD. However, any dates given at this time must be treated with the greatest of caution, and all that can be said is that the Midland Gaels were obviously able to establish themselves and consolidate their power base, for by the time Ireland moves into the 'historic' period proper, we find these particular Gaels involved in a gigantic struggle for control of the north of the island — the ancient province of Ulster.

The first Gaelic leader who bridges that twilight zone between 'purported' and 'actual' history is Niall Noígiallach, known as 'Niall of the Nine Hostages', whose mother was British. From him the greatest dynasty to emerge from among the Gaels, the Uí Néill, claim direct descent. (The Uí Néill would much later become synonymous with the long family line of powerful Gaelic chieftains, the O'Neills.)

Although at the time of Niall's reign — reckoned to be about the first quarter of the fifth century — Ireland was in the last phase of its unrecorded history, scholars find no reason to doubt his existence. While the middle of Ireland was still not secure to the Uí Néill — the ancient annals tell of battles between 475 and 516 before the Uí Néill conquered the plain of Mide — it appears that it was to the conquest of the North that Niall and his sons directed their first major efforts.

Ancient tradition has it that a few generations before the reign of Niall, three brothers, the 'Three Collas', relatives of the then king of Tara, Muiredach Tírech, first initiated the attack on Ulster, though some scholars now feel the actual invasion was the work of Niall and his sons, and took place during his reign.

> The Collas asked: 'what country dost thou of thy power the most readily assign us, that we make swordland of it? (for warriors better than the Collas there were none). Muiredach said: 'attack Ulster; they are not kindly disposed to us.' But yonder was a warrior force too great for the Collas; so they went to the men of Connacht, and became their protégés, and they received them. Subsequently Connacht came with them, seven battalions strong all told, and they were at the cairn of *Achadh lethderg* in Farney, in Ulster. From that cairn they deliver seven battles against Ulster, one daily to a week's end: being six fought by Connacht and one by the Collas. Every single day Ulster was routed; the Collas' battle was on the last day; recreant failure in fighting was none there; the battle was maintained for a summer's day and night, till blood reached shields; hard by the cairn is *coll na nothar* 'Hazel of the Wounded.' [In this last battle] Ulster gave way at break of the second day; the slaughter lasted as far as Glenree. A week then the others spent harrying Ulster, and they made swordland of the country. [28]

14

Ulster   At the time of Niall's attempt at conquest we do not know what type of internal political structure existed in Ulster. Previous to the attack on the North, the existence of the massive earthwork defences — the 'Great Wall' — hinted strongly at a definite regional demarcation, even political boundary, and in the prehistoric period the territory of Ulster may not only have embraced the whole north of the island but stretched as far south as the Boyne valley. There was probably a system of tribal alliances, and within this the dominant political grouping were the *Ulaid* (from whom 'Ulster' was to get its name) — the *Voluntii* mentioned on Ptolemy's map. The Ulaid, according to Francis Byrne, "most probably represented a warrior caste of La Tène Celts from Britain, wielding an overlordship over indigenous tribes." [24] Among these 'indigenous tribes', who obviously still formed the majority of the population, the most important and the most populous were the *Cruthin* (Pytheas' 'Pretani'). These pre-Celtic peoples shared in the over-kingship of Ulster, particular those Cruthin later known as the Dál nAraidi. The Cruthin more often than not bore the brunt of the wars against the Uí Néill, and at times claimed that it was they who were the *fír-Ulaid*, the 'true Ulstermen'.

In the far west of Ulster the Uí Neill conquest was the most complete, and the Ulster leaders there were driven east. Niall's sons, Connall, Eogan (Owen) and Enda, established their own kingdoms. The territory of Connall, now Donegal, became known as Tir-Connall (the Land of Connall), and from Connall were descended the O'Donnells. The territory of Owen was Inishowen (the Island of Owen). The Clan Owen later expanded into Tir Owen, which is now called Tyrone. From Owen descended the Northern O'Neills, the McLoughlins, O'Kanes, O'Hagans, O'Mullans, Devlins and other Gaelic planters. Niall's remaining sons stayed in control of the Midlands.

The capital of Ulster at Emain Macha seems to have either fallen to the Uí Néill, or been abandoned by the Ulstermen, around 450 AD.

In the southern and central part of Ulster a number of vassal tribes, known to us by the collective name of the Airgialla (Oriel) either took the opportunity to declare their autonomy or managed to co-exist precariously between the Uí Néill and the retreating Ulstermen.

The "Dane's Cast"   The boundary between Airgialla and the now-reduced territory of Ulster was made permanent by yet another massive earthwork wall, running along the vale of the Newry River (Glen Rige). It extended from Lisnagade one mile north-east of Scarva in County Down, to near Meigh, not far from Killeavy, and Slieve Gullion in Armagh. Parts of this earthwork, much later erroneously named "Dane's Cast", can still be seen to this day. In construction it consists of a wide fosse or trench with a rampart on either side. The numerous raths and duns on the eastern side, coupled with the vast quantity of ancient arms found in the vicinity, would seem to indicate that the area was densely populated by a strong military force. The chief fortifications were at Lisnagade, Fathom, Crown Mound, Tierney and Listullyard. Next to

Lisnagade, Fathom must have been the most important place since it commands Moiry Pass. This defence system was to remain politically effective for the next two hundred years.

However, excepting the permanent nature of the "Dane's Cast" fortifications, other parts of the new boundaries of Ulster were more fluid. As Francis Byrne commented: "It seems that the collapse of the Ulaid was not total nor regarded as irreversible. They may have occupied southern Louth well into the seventh century and their Cruthin associates were similarly tenacious in county Londonderry... The Ulaid certainly were to remain for many generations a much more powerful force than later historians of the Uí Néill high-kingship cared to remember." [24]

3 — The Ulster Sagas

Among the great works of early Irish literature are a group of tales known as the Ulster Cycle, traditionally felt to depict the North of Ireland in the first few centuries AD. While some scholars suggest that certain of the episodes enshrined within these tales have some bearing on actual historical events, this can only be speculation. The most we can say is that the whole structure of society as depicted in the sagas, the weapons and characteristics of the warriors, and their methods of warfare, agree precisely with the descriptions by classical authors of life among the Britons and Gauls before the Roman invasions. So, while we cannot take them as 'historical' evidence, these stories nevertheless give us a glimpse, albeit romanticised, into Ireland's Iron Age — its 'Heroic' Age — and are, moreover, a rich ingredient of this island's cultural heritage.

Emain Macha According to the sagas, the great citadel at Emain Macha contained within it three main buildings: that of the Red Branch, in which was kept the heads and arms of vanquished enemies; that of the Royal Branch, where the king lodged; and the Speckled House, in which were stored the swords, shields and spears of Ulster's warriors. The latter building received its name from the gold and silver of the shields, and the glint from all the weapons, stored there in order that, when quarrels arose at any of the banquets, the warriors would not have the means at hand to slay one another!

As Douglas Hyde wrote: "Conor's palace at Emania contained, according to the *Book of Leinster*, one hundred and fifty rooms, each large enough for three couples to sleep in, constructed of red oak, and bordered with copper. Conor's own chamber was decorated with bronze and silver, and ornamented with golden birds, in whose eyes were precious stones, and was large enough for thirty warriors to drink together in. Above the king's head hung his silver wand with three golden apples, and when he shook it silence reigned throughout the palace, so that even the fall of a pin might be heard. A large vat, always full of good drink, stood ever on the palace floor." [29]

An eighth-century law tract, *Críth Gablach*, gives a somewhat unrealistic summary of a king's duties: "There is moreover a weekly order proper for a king, i.e. Sunday for drinking ale, for he is no rightful prince who does not promise ale for every Sunday; Monday for legal business, for adjudicating between *tuatha* (tribes); Tuesday for chess; Wednesday for watching greyhounds racing; Thursday for marital intercourse; Friday for horse-racing; Saturday for judgements."

A place like Emain Macha would have been the venue for popular assemblies, which served not only as fairs and markets, but for the transaction of public business. These occasions were treated almost as holiday events, with horse-racing, feats of strength and various kinds of amusements on hand.

The 'Pangs' One of the legends as to how Emain Macha received its name
of Ulster relates to such a fair. Among the many spectators at a chariot race, in which the king's victorious chariot and horses greatly impressed the crowd, was a man who imprudently boasted that his wife was a faster charioteer. The hapless man was brought straightway before the king, who, when he had heard the proud boast, immediately sent for the unsuspecting woman. However, when the messenger located her, she protested that she was heavy with child and was in no fit state to race. The messenger informed her that in that case things did not augur well for her husband. The woman knew she had no choice but to accompany him. The expectant crowd clamoured for her to race, and it was in vain that she pleaded her condition to them. Finally she angrily told them that if they forced her to race, a long-lasting evil would fall upon the whole of Ulster. This still wasn't enough to deter the crowd and she was forced to commence the race. Just as her chariot reached the end of the field, she tumbled from it, and, right before the assembled spectators, gave birth to twins. At the height of her labour she screamed out that in times of greatest danger a debilitating illness — the 'pangs' — would seize the warriors of Ulster and leave them lying as helplessly unable to fight as she was now lying in her labour pains. The woman's name was Macha, and it is said that Emain Macha means the 'Twins of Macha'.

Cúchulainn, The Ulster sagas are full of larger than life characters,
Champion of Ulster both men and women. However, there is one who stands out above the others — the hero Cúchulainn, 'Champion of Ulster'. Born in the plain just south of what is now the Cooley Peninsula in County Louth, his boyhood name was Sétanta, a non-Gaelic name which is cognate with a tribe who lived in Lancashire, the Setantii, who are mentioned in Ptolemy's map of the British Isles. One tradition, preserved by Dubhaltach, relates that he belonged to a non-Gaelic tribe called Tuath Tabhairn. In the sagas it also states that he was not of the Ulaid, the Celtic ruling minority in Ulster: "The MS Harlean 5280 tells us categorically that Cú Chulaind was exempt from [the sickness of the Ulstermen], *ar nar bó don Ulltaib do*, 'for he was not of the Ulaid'."[30] Further, his physical appearance was quite at

variance with the physique of the Celts, for while they are usually described as tall, with long flowing fair hair, Cúchulainn is described as short in stature, with close-cropped dark hair, physical attributes more in keeping with the *pre*-Celtic inhabitants of Ireland. Finally, his inheritance, the plain of Muirthemne, was well-defined Cruthin territory. Now, given such an assortment of circumstantial evidence, it could well be speculated that the legend of Cúchulainn emanated from among the majority Cruthin population of Ulster. However, although such speculation is the daily and cherished practice of historians, for various reasons most have proven quite touchy in this case — perhaps it disturbs some long-established and jealously-guarded notions — so such speculation will not be indulged in here, and we will return to the hero's own story.

Filled with an urge to visit Emain Macha and meet the elite fighting force billeted there known as the Warriors of the Red Branch, young Sétanta finally made his farewell to his parents and journeyed to the great citadel. Once there he made an immediate impression on King Conor and his warriors, but not before he had experienced the first of many uncontrollable fits of rage which would overcome him in moments of anger, change his physical appearance alarmingly, and endow him with almost superhuman fighting capability. Indeed, such a fit came upon him after his first border encounter with the enemies of Ulster, and the only way the concerned citizens of Emain Macha were able to prevent many of their own number being counted among his victims was to send the women of Ulster out to meet him, all quite naked. Our hero's intense embarrassment caused him to falter, and this respite allowed the warriors to seize him and dissipate his rage by plunging him into vats of cold water.

His most famous deed while still a youth was one which would lead to a new name. Asked by Conor to accompany him on a visit to Culann the Smith, Sétanta accepted but requested that he be allowed to complete the game he was then engaged in. Conor agreed and told the youth to follow on behind. However, when the king and his retinue reached their host's dwelling and the latter ordered the gates of the surrounding palisade to be secured, Conor omitted to mention that a final member of his party was following. Once the gates were secured Culann released his massive guard dog, so powerful that it took three chains to restrain it, with three men on each chain.

The reader can guess what transpired next. Sétanta, arriving outside the palisade, was savagely attacked by the dog, but after a fierce and bloody struggle managed to kill it. Conor and his host had by this time arrived on the scene, and while everyone was delighted that the youth had not only survived, but shown such remarkable fighting ability, Culann was devastated by the loss of such a magnificent guard dog. In an attempt to make amends, Sétanta offered to act as guard in the dog's place, until such time as a pup of the same fierce breeding could be trained for the task. This suggestion was widely welcomed, and it was further pronounced that henceforth the young Sétanta would be known as 'Cú Chulainn', the 'Hound of Culann'.

However, Cúchulainn's greatest glory was to be accorded him after he had repelled a massive invasion force which threatened the very survival of Ulster itself.

The Táin   The ancient tale known as the *Táin Bó Cuailgne*, the 'Cattle-Raid of Cooley', is the masterpiece of Irish saga literature.[31] Indeed, it is the *oldest* vernacular story in Western European literature, and therefore holds an eminent place not only within the development of Irish literature, but within that of European literature as well.   Thomas Kinsella has pointed out: "The language of the earliest form of the story is dated to the eighth century, but some of the verse chapters may be two centuries older [and] must have had a long oral existence before [receiving] a literary shape."[32]

The story concerns an assault upon Ulster by the massed armies of the 'men of Ireland', led by Maeve, Queen of Connacht.   The bloody and bitter fighting that ensued has all the hallmarks of a full-scale invasion, and the appellation of 'cattle raid' hardly does justice to the carnage wrecked upon Ulster.   However, as Charles Doherty pointed out: "In this society cattle were the basis of the economy.   There was no coinage before the Norse began to mint in the late tenth century, and cattle were used as the main units of value.   The constant cattle-raiding which took place was the parry and thrust of politics."[33]   Francis Byrne also commented: "As tribute was usually reckoned in cattle, the 'wars' tended to be primarily cattle-raids."[24]

No sooner were Maeve's armies making their advance into the North than the fighting men of Ulster were afflicted with their 'pangs' and could offer no resistance.   Cúchulainn, who, as we have already seen, was unaffected by this debility, had to defend his homeland single-handedly.   While the story then concentrates on the gigantic and bloody one-sided battle that now raged (one-sided, that is, from the point of view of the invaders, for their ranks were steadily decimated by Ulster's hero), the saga also brings in a very tragic episode — the combat between Cúchulainn and his southern foster-brother, Ferdia.   Unlike the approach taken with the other battle sequences, where blood and heads fly as a matter of course and where humanitarian considerations seem remote, the story of this combat between the two men is described with great emotion, pathos, even tenderness.   While this pathos is undoubtedly directed at the tragedy of two foster-brothers thus locked in mortal combat, nevertheless the episode is a remarkably moving depiction of the absurdity and futility of man's preoccupation with violence and killing.

Finally King Conor managed to raise himself from his 'pangs' and summoned his warriors with a rousing battle oration: "As the sky is above us, the earth beneath us and the sea all around us, I swear that unless the sky with all its stars should fall upon the earth, or the ground burst open in an earthquake, or the sea sweep over the land, we shall never retreat one inch, but shall gain victory in battle and return every woman to her family and every cow to its byre."

Soon, as Queen Maeve scanned the plain before her, she saw a great grey mist which filled the void between heaven and earth, with what seemed like sifted snow falling down, above which flew a multitude of birds, and all this accompanied by a great clamour and uproar. One of Maeve's warriors turned to her. "The grey mist we see is the fierce breathing of the horses and heroes, the sifted snow is the foam and froth being cast from the horses' bits, and the birds are the clods of earth flung up by the horses' dashing hoves."

"It matters little," retorted Maeve, "we have good warriors with which to oppose them."

"I wouldn't count on that," replied the warrior, "for I assure you you won't find in all Ireland or Alba a host which can oppose the Ulstermen once their fits of wrath come upon them."

The warrior's prediction was quite accurate, for Maeve's armies were completely routed and fled in disarray, Maeve herself only escaping death through Cúchulainn's personal intervention.

Cúchulainn's Maeve never forgave Cúchulainn the humiliation she and her
Last Battle army had suffered as a result of their inglorious incursion into
Ulster. Even his sparing of her life was immaterial to her intense desire for revenge.

Conor, suspecting that Maeve was plotting the Champion's downfall, ordered him to be sent into seclusion, but Maeve, calling upon the dark arts of magic, had his mind so bewitched he hallucinated that his enemies were once again invading and despoiling his homeland. Cúchulainn's wife, Emer, realising that things were greatly amiss with her beloved, redoubled her efforts to restrain him from dashing out of Emain Macha to do battle. Despite being reassured that his visions were unreal phantoms, they persisted, and finally Cúchulainn managed to slip away from the security of his friends, having convinced his loyal charioteer, Laeg, to accompany him.

Cúchulainn then encountered a series of ill omens, and realised that events were rapidly taking him to his final destiny. His enemies were drawn up, in full battle array, their chosen battleground Cúchulainn's ancestral territory — Mag Muirthemne. Once more, Cúchulainn proved why he inspired so much terror in the hearts of his enemies.

> He played equally with spear, shield, and sword, he performed all the feats of a warrior. As many as there are of grains of sand in the sea, of stars in the heaven, of dewdrops in May, of snowflakes in winter, of hailstones in a storm, or leaves in a forest, of ears of corn in the plains of Bregia, of sods beneath the feet of the steeds of Erin on a summer's day, so many halves of heads, and halves of shields, and halves of hands and halves of feet, so many red bones were scattered by him throughout the plain of Muirthemne, it became grey with the brains of his enemies, so fierce and furious was Cúchulainn's onslaught.[29]

However, with his enemies now being aided by the sinister forces of magic, the outcome was inevitable. Three of Cúchulainn's bitterest enemies confronted him with a spear which they were told had magical powers and would that day lay low a king. The first throw, however, instead of piercing Cúchulainn, killed his faithful companion, Laeg — the 'king' of charioteers. Furious, his assailants threw again, but this time it was the Champion's noble steed, the Grey of Macha — the 'king' of steeds — which received a mortal wound and galloped off. The third throw finally struck Cúchulainn, causing a terrible injury to his stomach.

The fatally-wounded Champion struggled over to a tall stone and tied himself to it, so that he could die standing. As his enemies edged closer, still in awe of this great warrior, Cúchulainn's dying but ever-faithful steed returned once more to his side, scattering the advancing foes with terrible charges into their ranks. It was all to no avail, and Cúchulainn's enemies sensed that victory was finally to be theirs. Yet, even after one of them smote off the Champion's head, Cúchulainn's sword, falling now from his lifeless arm, severed the hand of his assailant.

As his enemies rejoiced and celebrated their great victory around the dead hero, his lifelong friend Conall Cearnach came upon the scene, and in a terrible fit of anger exacted a fierce revenge, before finally carrying the body of his companion back to Emain Macha.

Emer, on seeing her dead husband, was smitten with intense grief.

> She washed clean the head and she joined it on to its body, and she pressed it to her heart and her bosom, and fell to lamenting and heavily sorrowing over it, and she placed around the head a lovely satin cloth. 'Ochone!' said she, 'good was the beauty of this head, although it is low this day, and it is many of the kings and princes of the world would be keening it if they thought it was like this. Love of my soul, O friend, O gentle sweetheart, and O thou one choice of the men of the earth, many is the woman envied me thee until now, and I shall not live after thee', and her soul departed out of her, and she herself and Cúchulainn were laid in the one grave by Conall, and he raised their stone over their tomb, and he wrote their names in Ogam, and their funeral games were performed by him and the Ultonians.[29]

Déirdre of the Sorrows   This brief résumé of the richness of the Ulster Tales would be incomplete without mention of one of the oldest stories of romance, adventure and treachery in Western European literature — the story of the 'Fate of the Children of Usnach', more popularly known as 'Déirdre of the Sorrows' after the play by J. M. Synge.

It so happened that King Conor and some of his warriors were feasting at the home of his chief storyteller, when their host's wife gave birth to a girl. This was seen as cause for even more celebration, and the king's seer, Cathbad, was called upon to prophesy the child's future. The child, he said, would grow up to have exceptional physical qualities: curling golden hair, green eyes of great beauty, cheeks flushed like the foxglove, teeth white as pearls and a tall, perfectly shaped body. However, the pleasure of the assembled gathering was immediately dissipated when the seer continued with his prophecy. This child, because of her very great beauty, and the intense jealously it would cause, would bring a terrible evil upon the whole of Ulster, which would result in untold suffering and countless graves.

The warriors of Ulster were horrified and clamoured that the only way to avert such a tragedy would be to have the child slain. Conor, perhaps with feeling for his host and his distraught wife, but no doubt also with his shrewd eye on an opportunity not to be missed, announced that the child would be allowed to live, but to prevent the predicted jealousy, and thereby avert the threatened doom, he himself would take the girl to be his wife when she came of age.

So it was that Déirdre was reared by her nurse in a secluded part of the king's palace, where no man, other than her tutor or the king, was permitted to set foot. As she grew up, her physical beauty proved to be everything that Cathbad had prophesied.

However, one day her tutor killed a young calf, and as it lay on the snow a raven came to drink the blood. Déirdre turned to her nurse and said, "The only man I could love would be one who should have those three colours, hair black as the raven, cheeks red as the blood, body white as the snow." Her nurse revealed that there was such a young man living in Emain Macha — Naisi, one of the three sons of Usnach. So great was Déirdre's desire to see this youth that she convinced her nurse to arrange a seemingly innocent encounter while he was out walking.

The young pair fell instantly in love, although Naisi was too mindful at first of incurring Conor's wrath to want to get too involved. But the dictates of love, and Déirdre's own pleadings, soon got the better of his fears, and one night the couple slipped away in the darkness, accompanied by Naisi's two brothers. Realising that Conor would hunt the length and breadth of Ulster for the fugitives, the youthful party finally departed for Scotland.

However, Déirdre's beauty attracted male attention once again, and the couple had to keep on the move, continually harassed by the men of Scotland, until they managed to set up home in the beautiful Glen Etive.

As time passed many were those who counselled Conor to forgive the exiles their insult to him, saying it would be a tragedy for three sons of Ulster to die at the hand of enemies abroad. The aging king finally agreed to send messengers to bid them return home. These emissaries convinced Naisi and his brothers that all was forgiven and it was safe to return, though Déirdre remained disbelieving.

The group finally journeyed to Ulster, to be met by their good friend Fergus, one of the most respected warriors of the Red Branch. It was his promise to watch over them — and his threat to kill anyone who harmed them — that had finally helped persuade them to return. But Conor, by trickery, managed to divert Fergus from his task, and the party were entrusted to the protection of Fergus' two sons. As the omens of evil gradually grew thicker, Déirdre's premonition of treachery intensified.

> O Naisi, view the cloud
> That I see here on the sky,
> I see over Emania green
> A chilling cloud of blood-tinged red.[29]

Upon their arrival at Emain Macha, instead of being admitted to the king's own lodgings, they were accommodated in the House of the Red Branch, on the pretence that it was better stocked with food and drink for strangers. The party realised now that all was far from well.

Late that night Conor, still fired with his jealously, asked Déirdre's old nurse to find out if her former charge still retained her great beauty. The nurse, after warning the young couple that Conor was a great threat to their safety, returned to the king and tried to convince him that time had indeed taken its toll of Déirdre's looks, with much of her beauty now lost. This seemed to satisfy Conor for a while, but, being suspicious of the report, he sent another retainer to ascertain the truth. This spy finally found a chink in the barred windows and doors of the House of the Red Branch and observed the two lovers within. They in turn spotted him and angrily flung a chess piece which put out his eye. The injured man hurried back to Conor, telling the king that it was worth losing an eye to have beheld a woman so lovely.

Conor straightway gathered together a force of men and began an assault on the House of the Red Branch. By the dawn, although one of Fergus' sons lay slain in his attempt to defend his charges, the three sons of Usnach were captured and beheaded. Déirdre's lament over her lover's dead body is one of the masterpieces of early Irish tragic verse, and was much rewritten by Irish scribes.

> Naisi is laid in his tomb.
> sad was the protection that he got;
> the nation by which he was reared poured out
> the cup of poison by which he died.

> His ruddy cheeks, more beautiful than meadows,
> red lips, eyebrows of the colour of the chafer,
> his teeth shining like pearls
> like noble colour of snow.

> Break not to-day my heart (O Conor!),
> soon I shall reach my early grave,
> stronger than the sea is my grief
> dost thou not know it, O Conor?[34]

When Fergus heard of the treachery and Conor's subsequent abduction of Déirdre, he and many other outraged Red Branch warriors fell upon Emain

Macha and killed three hundred of those who remained loyal to Conor, as well as many women and members of Conor's own family. Then they burned Emain Macha and departed into exile, a full three thousand of them. Taking up service with their former adversary, Queen Maeve of Connacht, they made continual raids upon their former homeland, killing and despoiling in revenge for the murder of the sons of Usnach.

As for Déirdre, she never smiled again, and Conor, finally tiring of this, in annoyance asked her what she hated most. To which question she named the king himself and one of his closest retainers. "Well then," said the vindictive Conor, "I shall send you to his couch for a year." As Conor rode out the next day, with Déirdre behind him in the chariot, she suddenly flung herself onto the ground, and dashing her head against a rock was instantly killed.

While these sagas are believed to describe an Ulster of the first few centuries AD, and probably had a long oral existence, they only took literary form in the eighth and ninth centuries. However, the development of Irish writing which made this flowering of culture possible was to be proceeded by the introduction into Ireland of a new and powerful force which was to have a fundamental impact on the Irish peoples and their history.

The ancient *Annals of Ulster* record two significant events, occurring one year apart:

> In the year 431 from the Incarnation of the Lord, Palladius, ordained by Celestinus, bishop of the city of Rome, is sent, in the consulship of Etius and Valerius, into Ireland, first bishop to the Scots (Irish), that they might believe in Christ."

> "AD 432. Patrick arrived at Ireland, in the 9th year of the reign of Theodosius the younger, in the first year of the episcopate of Xistus, the 42nd bishop of the Church of Rome."[35]

Ireland's period of 'ancient' history was now at an end — an new era was about to begin.

Medieval

432 — 1381

1 — 'Light of the World'

The Arrival of   In 398 AD St Ninian had established the first Christian
Christianity   Church in what is now Scotland at Candida Casa (now
Whithorn) in Galloway. Although little is known about this
great Christian Saint of the Novantes, or the earliest history of his foundation,
it is clear that in the fifth and sixth centuries Candida Casa was an important
centre of evangelism to both Britain and the northern part of Ireland.

To the Irish, however, the main credit for the introduction of Christianity to
Ireland belongs to St Patrick. Yet, despite Patrick's pre-eminent place in the
history of the Irish Church, we do not know just how much of his story is
historically accurate. Ironically, the only first-hand accounts of Patrick come
from two works which he reputedly wrote himself, the *Confession* and the
Epistle to Coroticus. Further, the reference to his arrival in the Annals cannot
be taken as necessarily factual either, as it is now believed that the Annals only
became contemporary in the latter part of the sixth century, and fifth century
entries were therefore 'backdated'. The question of Palladius and his mission
from Rome leads to still more uncertainty, with some scholars even proposing
the idea that there could have been 'two' Patricks. Francis Byrne suggested
that "we may suspect that some of the seventh-century traditions originally
referred to Palladius and have been transferred, whether deliberately or as a
result of genuine confusion, to the figure of Patrick." [24]

This uncertainty must be borne in mind when we come to look at his story.
Patrick was first brought to Ireland as a slave from Romanised Britain and sold
to a Cruthinic chieftain called Milchu, who used him to tend flocks around
Mount Slemish in County Antrim. After six years of servitude he managed to
escape from Ireland, first going by boat to the Continent, then two years later
returning to his parents in Britain. Despite his parents being anxious that he
would now remain at home, Patrick had a vision of an angel who had come
from Ireland with letters, in one of which was relayed the message: "We beg
you, Holy youth, to come and walk amongst us once again." To Patrick, the
letters "completely broke my heart and I could read no more and woke up."

Tradition tells that Patrick eventually made the journey back to Ireland,
finally landing in County Down in the territory of Dichu (of the Ulaid) who
became his first convert. Dichu's barn (sabhall or Saul) near Downpatrick was
the first of his churches.

Among Patrick's first converts were Bronagh, daughter of Milchu, and her
son Mochaoi (Mahee). St Mochaoi was to found the great monastery of
Nendrum on Mahee Island in Loch Cuan (Strangford Lough), and is associated
with the saint in the legends which grew around Patrick's name. These legends
firmly place Down as the cradle of Christianity in Ireland. At Nendrum were
first educated Colman, who was of the Cruthin, and Finnian, who was of the

Ulaid. Colman founded in the early sixth century the famous See of Dromore in Iveagh, while Finnian, following a visit to Candida Casa, founded the great school of Movilla (Newtownards) in Down. Finnian is also notable for bringing the first copy of the Scriptures to Ireland.

Patrick himself is said to have founded Armagh around 444, and the selection of a site so close to Emain Macha would strongly suggest that the Ulster capital was still the most powerful over-kingdom in Ireland at that time.

Not everyone was necessarily overjoyed to see the return of Patrick. His old master Milchu, a convinced pagan, when forewarned of an impending visit by Patrick, set fire to his house and all his property, then perished in the flames rather than risk being converted! Nor was every conversion lasting — King Laeghaire, despite being baptised, remained pagan at heart and was buried at his own request with pagan rites. Estyn Evans wrote that "Professor R.A.S. Macalister of University College, Dublin, a Gaelic enthusiast turned cynic, used to say in private that the number of believing Christians in the early centuries of Christianity could probably be reckoned by counting the number of Irish saints." [10]

Certainly the Elder Faiths of the ordinary people remained extremely strong, forcing the Church to incorporate many of the manifestations of these ancient beliefs — rites concerning spring wells, sacred stones and trees, wakes for the dead — into the new religion. As W.G. Wood-Martin wrote: "Christianity is generally supposed to have annihilated heathenism in Ireland. In reality it merely smoothed over and swallowed its victim, and the contour of its prey, as in the case of the boa-constrictor, can be distinctly traced under the glistening colours of its beautiful skin. Paganism still exists, it is merely inside instead of outside." [12]

Comgall and Bangor   Most of the early monastic settlements would have been quite basic arrangements — Cardinal Thomás O Fiaich said we should picture them like modern holiday camps, with rows of wooden accommodation chalets grouped around a few central activity buildings.[36]

By far the most important of these settlements was Bangor, founded in 555 on Ulidian territory by Comgall, perhaps the most famous of all the Cruthin. The name 'Bangor' comes from the medieval *Beannchar*, which may mean 'pointed arrangement', possibly referring to the pointed sticks in the wattled fence which would have surrounded the settlement. It was Bangor which would give the largest number of great names to Irish religious history, figures such as Columbanus, Gall, Moluag, Maelrubha, Dungal and Malachy.

Comgall, it is said, was born at Magheramorne, County Antrim, in 512. Having shown great promise in his early years of a vocation to the Christian ministry, Comgall was educated under St Fintan at Clonenagh, and is also said to have studied under Finnian at Clonard and Mobhi Clairenach at Glasnevin. Following his ordination as a deacon and priest, Comgall was imbued with a great missionary zeal and founded many cells or monasteries before finally establishing Bangor on the coast of County Down. To distinguish it from the other Bangors in the British Isles it became known as Bangor Mór, 'Bangor the Great'. The monastic settlement consisted of a large number of huts made of wattles situated around the church or oratory with its refectory, school, scriptorium and hospice. The whole establishment was surrounded by a vallum which consisted of a rampart and ditch. Life at Bangor was very severe. The food was sparse and even milk was considered an indulgence. Only one meal per day was allowed and that not until evening. Confession was held in public before the whole community and severe acts of penance were observed. There was silence at meal times and at other times conversation was restricted to the minimum. Comgall himself was extremely pious and austere and it is said that he arose in the middle of the night to recite psalms and say prayers while immersed in the nearby stream.

The strength of the community lay in its form of worship. The choral services were based on the antiphonal singing from Gaul, introduced into the West by Ambrose of Milan in the fourth century. Bangor became famous for this type of choral psalmody and it spread from there throughout Europe once more. The glory of Bangor was the celebration of a perfected and refined *Laus Perennis* and in singing this the community of Bangor entered into a covenant of mutual love and service in the Church of Jesus Christ. Because of the great number of students and monks attached to Bangor and its outlying daughter churches, it was possible to have a continuous chorus of the Divine Praise sung by large choirs which were divided into groups, each of which took regular duty and sang with a refinement not possible when St Martin was organising the raw recruits of Gaul.

The Bangor Antiphonary One of the most important religious works produced at Bangor was the *Bangor Antiphonary*, now housed in the Ambrosian Library of Milan. The creed found in this work differs in wording from all others known and is in substance the original Creed of Nicaea. For this reason alone the *Bangor Antiphonary* may be considered one of the most precious relics of Western civilisation. 'Correct' belief, the now standard orthodoxy of the Christian Church, was established chiefly at the First Ecumenical Council of Nicaea (now Iznik in Turkey) in May 325 AD. The resultant Nicene Creed was an enlarged and explanatory version of the Apostles' Creed in which the doctrines of Christ's divinity and of the Holy Trinity were defined.

In the *Antiphonary*, there is a celebration of Bangor's contribution to church history:

The Holy, valiant deeds
Of sacred Fathers,
Based on the matchless
Church of Bangor;

The noble deeds of abbots,
Their number, times and names,
Of never-ending lustre,
Hear, brothers; great their deserts,
> Whom the Lord hath gathered
> To the mansions of his heavenly kingdom.
Christ loved Comgall,
Well, too, did he the Lord.

There is also a hymn to Comgall himself:

Let us remember the shining justice of our patron, St Comgall, glorious in deed, aided by the spirit of God and, by the holy and radiant light of the sublime Trinity, directing all things under his rule...

Listen, everyone, to the deeds of this champion of God, who has been introduced to the secrets of the angels. From the first flowering of his youth his uprightness, strengthened by his faith, was nourished on the pages of the Law and was introduced to the joys of God. The virtues which he showed in his great life were abundantly in keeping with his faith...

He set himself like a barrier of iron in front of the people to rout, to uproot and destroy all evil and to build and implant good for the benefit of all, like St Hieremia set on high...[38]

Comgall, by all accounts, was a commanding personality. "Such was his reputation for piety and learning that multitudes flocked to his school from the most distant parts; it is well established that not less than 3,000 students and teachers were under his care at one time, including many of the most honourable in the land. The evangelistic zeal of Comgall was pre-eminent — down to the landing-place at the reef of rocks he led many a band of his disciples who were to embark on their frail coracles to spread the Gospel in European countries." [39]

Cradle of Irish Literature At Bangor were compiled in all probability the original Chronicles of Ireland, and the beautiful poetry *The Voyage of Bran*. In this region too the old traditions of Ulster were preserved and these were moulded into the Gaelic masterpiece the *Táin Bó Cuailgne* (Cattle Raid of Cooley). The ancient 'Ulster Chronicle', from which it is believed the oldest entries in the *Annals of Ulster* were derived, has been attributed to Sinlan Moccu Min, who is described in the lists of abbots in the *Bangor Antiphonary* as the "famed teacher of the world" (famosus mundi magister).

Proinsias Mac Cana has summed up the rich cultural legacy of this region of Ulster: "In Ireland the seventh century was marked by two closely related developments: the rapid extension of the use of writing in the Irish language and an extraordinary quickening of intellectual and artistic activity which was to continue far beyond the limit of the century. The immediate sources of this artistic renewal were the scriptoria of certain of the more progressive monasteries and its direct agents those monastic *literati* whom the Irish metrical tracts refer to by the significant title of *nualitride*, 'new men of *letters*'. While there is no reason to suppose that these individuals were confined to any one part of the country, nevertheless the evidence strongly suggests that it was only in the east, or more precisely in the south-east, of Ulster that their activities assumed something of the impetus and cohesiveness of a cultural movement. Here conservation and creativity went hand in hand: the relatively new skill of writing in the vernacular began to be vigorously exploited not only for the direct recording of secular oral tradition — heroic, mythological and the more strictly didactic — but also at the same time as a vehicle for the imaginative re-creation of certain segments of that tradition, so that one may with due reservations speak of this region of south-east Ulster as the cradle of written Irish literature... Bangor seems to have been the intellectual centre whence the cultural dynamic of the east Ulster region emanated." [40]

Columba   One of the great religious figures of Ireland was Columba (Columb-Cille) a prince of the Northern Uí Néill; his father, it is said, being the great-grandson of Niall of the Nine Hostages. Columba studied under St Finnian at Movilla, where he was ordained deacon, and, according to the *Annals of Ulster*, founded Derry in 545. He became a close friend of Comgall's, even though the political and ethnic rivalries between their respective kinsmen must at times have sorely tested their shared Christianity.

Columba's biographer, Adamnan, the ninth abbot of Iona from 679-704, describes such an incident which highlights the communal conflicts of the period:

> At another time [Columba] and the abbot Comgall sit down not far from the fortress [of Cethirn], on a bright summer's day. Then water is brought to the Saints in a brazen vessel from a spring hard by, for them to wash their hands. Which when St Columba had received, he thus speaks to the abbot Comgall, who is sitting beside him: 'The day will come, O Comgall, when that spring, from which has come the water now brought to us, will not be fit for any human purposes.' 'By what cause,' says Comgall, 'will its spring water be corrupted?' Then says St Columba, 'Because it will be filled with human blood, for my family friends and thy relations according to the flesh, that is, the Uí Néill and the Cruthin people, will wage war, fighting in this fortress of Cethirn close by. Whence in the above-named spring some poor fellow of my kindred will be slain, and the basin of the same spring will be filled with the blood of him that is slain with the rest.' Which true prophecy of his was fulfilled in its season after many years. [41]

The saint's legend would have us believe that it was these political and ethnic distractions which finally persuaded Columba to leave Ireland and set up a new community out of sight of its shores. Yet although Columba had not stood aloof from political intrigue, or even inciting warfare, such involvement would not have been exceptional for the clergy at that time, some of whom carried weapons to the synods.

As J. T. Fowler wrote: "It is no marvel then if Columba, a leading spirit in the great clan of the northern Uí Néill, incited his kinsmen to fight about matters which would be felt most keenly as closely touching their tribal honour. But at the same time, such a man as he was may very well, upon calm reflection, have considered that his enthusiasm and energies would be more worthily bestowed on missionary work than in maintaining the dignity of his clan." [42]

Whatever the reasons for his departure, the history of the Church was to be so much the richer, for the community he founded, on the small island of Iona, close to the coast of Argyll, was destined to be the cultural apotheosis of Scotland, and the place where some scholars believe the magnificent *Book of Kells* was executed.

Columbanus The northern Irish monastic settlements, whether their influence emanated from Bangor or Iona, were not only to be directly responsible for the spread of Christianity to Scotland and northern England, but were to carry their missionary zeal to the very heart of Europe itself. Of all the numerous personalities who sought "to renounce home and family like Abraham and seek a secluded spot where the ties of the world would not interfere with their pursuit of sanctity" [36] none stands out more prominently among these *peregrini* than Columbanus.

Columbanus, it is said, was born of the old Leinster Cruthin, about the year 543. His biography was written on the continent in the last monastery he himself founded, and while it contains much detail of his career in Europe, it is sparing with facts about his youth in Ireland, and in it, as with all such documents, fact and fiction are no doubt well enmeshed.

The legend has it that when still a young man he decided to enter the religious life, and fearful that the ties of matrimony might prevent this — for he was reputedly a handsome youth who had already attracted female admirers — he decided to leave home for ever and go north to Ulster. When his mother tried to dissuade him from departing by throwing herself down across the threshold, Columbanus strode over her prostrate body. It is unlikely that he ever saw her again.

He travelled first to the island of Cleenish on Lough Erne where he received his early education under the celebrated scholar Sinell. His strength of purpose was that required by Comgall of his monks and so it was natural that Columbanus should come to the Cruthinic foundation at Bangor where he remained for many years as a disciple and friend of Comgall.

In 589 Columbanus set off from Bangor on what was to become one of the great missionary journeys of history. With him he had twelve companions, including his devoted friend, Gall.

Barbarian Europe   The European Continent on which Columbanus and his party set foot had experienced radical change. The Roman Empire and its widespread organisational network had disintegrated under the impact of the barbarian invasions, and now, instead of Roman proconsuls, barbarian kings and dukes established their rule over Europe. Under the first surge of these 'barbarians', not only had the Roman system of government disappeared, but order and learning had virtually collapsed and the practice of Christianity had been almost completely extinguished. Ireland, however, had not only been unaffected by these barbarian invasions, but had only been indirectly touched by Roman 'civilisation', which, in the rest of Europe had brought, alongside its beneficial aspects, an equally ruthless 'barbarianism' in its suppression of older European cultures. So not only had the Church survived intact in Ireland, but its traditions of learning had continued unimpaired.

In 590 the small group of missionaries arrived in the Merovingian kingdom of Burgundy, where Gunthram, king of Burgundy and Austrasia, received them warmly and established them at a place called Annegray which was the site of a derelict Roman castle. Here the monks repaired the ruined Temple of Diana and made it into their first church, rededicating it to St Martin of Tours. The king offered them every appreciation in terms of food and money but they declined, preferring to keep to the monastic ideals to which their lives were committed. Columbanus himself was wont to walk deep into the Burgundian forest, heedless of either starvation or danger, taking with him only the Bible he had transcribed in his beloved Bangor.

The king's ready support need not surprise us. Although the initial barbarian population movements had destroyed the existing Roman system, the barbarian chiefs still held the empire in awe. Christianity not only carried with it the great prestige of Roman civilisation, but consisted of a more coherent body of doctrine than the vast assortment of pagan gods, and therefore offered more advantages, both personal and political, to the newly emerging ruling elites. This soon encouraged a gradual revival of the dormant church.

Luxeuil   As the number of monks in the monastery at Annegray increased daily, it became necessary for the community to seek a more suitable site. King Gunthram had died in 593 and young Childebert II now ruled over Burgundy and Austrasia. His permission was given to build a second monastery eight miles west of Annegray, beside the River Breuchin, among the ruins of the former Roman fort at Luxovium, which had been completely destroyed by Attila and his Huns in 451. Here at the foot of the Vosges mountains, close by a healing stream, there arose the great Community of Luxeuil. Although the site had been completely deserted and overgrown, this exactly suited Columbanus, for he loved manual labour as much as he loved solitude. So great did the community here become that the noble youths of the Franks asked to be admitted to its brotherhood, and eventually it was necessary to establish a third foundation at Fontaine, three miles north of Luxeuil. (In fact, Luxeuil was to influence directly or indirectly nearly one hundred other religious foundations before the year 700.)

The community of Columbanus was now growing so large it became necessary to draw up written rules for the guidance of the monks. These rules were no doubt modelled on the *Good Rule of Bangor* written by Comgall. These rules covered everything from timetables for the recitation of psalms to instructions for obedience, fasting, and daily chanting. Some of the régime must seem harsh and authoritarian to us today, particularly the punishments to be meted out for infringements of the rules, these punishments usually being inflicted with a leather strap on the palm of the hand:

> The monk who does not prostrate himself to ask a prayer when leaving the house, and after receiving a blessing does not bless himself, and go to the cross — it is prescribed to correct him with twelve blows.
>
> The monk who will eat without a blessing — with twelve blows.
>
> The monk who through coughing goes wrong in the chant at the beginning of a psalm — it is laid down to correct him with six blows.
>
> The one who smiles at the synaxis, that is, at the office of prayers — with six blows; if he bursts out laughing aloud — with a grave penance unless it happens excusably.
>
> The one who receives the blessed bread with unclean hands — with twelve blows.[43]

Some of the rules showed a more insightful approach: "The talkative is to be punished with silence, the restless with the practice of gentleness, the gluttonous with fasting, the sleepy with watching, the proud with imprisonment, the deserter with expulsion."

While such rules of discipline show that Columbanus was strict in his approach to organising the daily life of his monasteries — and he was just as strict with himself — he was also well known for his warmth and understanding. His thoughtfulness about human relationships is shown in this letter he wrote to a young disciple:

> Be helpful when you are at the bottom of the ladder and be the lowest when you are in authority. Be simple in faith but well trained in manners; demanding in your own affairs but unconcerned in those of others. Be guileless in friendship, astute in the face of deceit, tough in time of ease, tender in hard times. Disagree where necessary, but be in agreement about truth. Be slow to anger, quick to learn, also slow to speak, as St James says, equally quick to listen. Be up and doing to make progress, slack to take revenge, careful in word, eager in work. Be friendly with men of honour, stiff with rascals, gentle to the weak, firm to the stubborn, steadfast to the proud, humble to the lowly. Be ever sober, ever chaste, ever modest. Be patient as far as compatible with zeal, never greedy, always generous, if not in money, then in spirit.[43]

34

Luxeuil quickly became the most celebrated monastery in Christendom after Bangor itself. Both sacred and classical studies were of the utmost importance. The art of music was prominent as in Bangor and was taught at a level at that time unknown in Europe. H. Zimmer has written: "They were the instructors in every branch of science and learning of the time, possessors and bearers of a higher culture than was at that time to be found anywhere on the Continent, and can surely claim to have been the pioneers — to have laid the cornerstone of western culture on the Continent."[44]

Expulsion Columbanus' penitential discipline and his independence of action infringed upon the powers of the local Frankish bishops, and he probably had few friends among them. When he insisted on celebrating Easter according to the Irish calculations he was accused of unorthodoxy, and relationships between him and the bishops deteriorated still further. Matters finally came to a head when he incurred the displeasure of the secular rulers also. Theuderich, the new young king of Burgundy, although married, installed concubines in the royal household, and soon had four illegitimate children. When the king's grandmother, Brunhilde, instructed Columbanus to confirm her grandson's illegitimate children, he refused, and from then on she was to prove his bitter enemy.

This confrontation may have been embellished somewhat by Columbanus' biographer, for, as Ian Wood points out, Columbanus "was not the first to criticise Merovingian concubinage; it would, in fact, be curious if an Irishman, coming from an island where royal concubinage was even more entrenched than in Francia, had been the first to condemn the practice."[45]

Whatever the actual details, in 610 Brunhilde succeeded in having Columbanus expelled from his beloved monastery, never to see it again. He and his party of Irish monks then embarked on a 600 mile journey westwards to the coast. Once there, they boarded a vessel which was to take them back to Ireland. However, a great storm arose and drove the boat back to the shore, where for the next three days it then became becalmed. The captain, believing all these events were a sign from God that he was not to co-operate in the expulsion of the Irish monks, set them back onto the shore again.

Another great journey now lay ahead of Columbanus and his party, made longer by the need to take a wide detour whereby they would avoid contact with their Burgundian adversaries. Finally, after much hardship they established their new headquarters close to Lake Constance at Bregenz (which lies in present-day Austria close to its borders with Switzerland and Germany). Here they built a small cloistered monastery, laid out a garden and planted fruit trees. But nature proved more yielding to their efforts than the local people, many of whom were deeply resentful of these intruders who had the effrontery to smash their pagan images and throw them into the lake. When some of the monks were murdered Columbanus realised that once again he must uproot himself and his community and seek elsewhere for a sanctuary.

However, not all his monks were prepared to embark on further travel into the unknown, including Gall, who throughout these years of hardship had probably been Columbanus' closest companion. When Gall broke the news to his aging friend, their parting must have been one of the most sorrowful occasions in both their lives.

Bobbio Although by now more than seventy years of age, Columbanus crossed the snow-covered Alps through the St Gothard's pass and made his way to the court of the Lombard king, who granted him a suitable place, at Bobbio, where he could found a new monastery. Columbanus was to die a year later but Bobbio was to grow in stature, attracting some of the finest scholars of the time and containing a splendid library of over 700 books.

Before he died Columbanus sent a messenger to seek out his old friend Gall, to let him know that the bitterness of their parting had been finally set aside. The great emperor Charlemagne was to build one of his most famous foundations

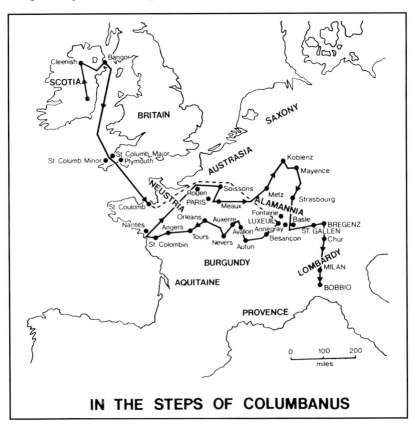

IN THE STEPS OF COLUMBANUS

— the Monastery of St Gall — near the spot where Columbanus' old travelling companion had lived the austere life of a hermit. A modern monastery now stands there today, of which it has been written: "The monastery... has in its library beautiful Irish manuscripts made by some of these travelling scholars. The library has also preserved a fine plan of Charlemagne's monastery with its sties and stables, its sheepfolds and fowl houses, threshing floors and market gardens... As well as this farm neatly laid out in a great rectangle around the central church, the monastery of St Gall had a hostel and a kitchen for its guests, schools and accommodation for the abbot and his monks, a doctor's clinic, an infirmary and a cemetery. Such settlements formed the high culture of Europe in the reign of Charlemagne." [46]

"Patron Saint of Europe" G.S.M. Walker wrote of Columbanus: "A character so complex and so contrary, humble and haughty, harsh and tender, pedantic and impetuous by turns, had as its guiding and unifying pattern the ambition of sainthood. All his activities were subordinate to that one end and with the self-sacrifice that can seem so close to self-assertion he worked out his sole salvation by the wondrous pathway that he knew. He was a missionary through circumstance, a monk by vocation, a contemplative, too frequently driven to action by the world, a pilgrim on the road to Paradise." [47] Pope Pius XI has said, "The more light that is shed by scholars in the period known as the Middle Ages the clearer it becomes that it was thanks to the initiative and labours of Columbanus that the rebirth of Christian virtue and civilisation over a great part of Gaul, Germany and Italy took place." The French poet Leon Cathlin concurs in saying, "He is, with Charlemagne, the greatest figure of our Early Middle Ages," and Daniel-Rops of the French Academy has also said that he was "a sort of prophet of Israel, brought back to life in the sixth century, as blunt in his speech as Isaias or Jeremias... For almost fifty years souls were stirred by the influence of St Columbanus. His passing through the country started a real contagion of holiness."

More recently, Robert Schuman, the French Foreign Minister who was a driving force behind the establishment of the European Economic Community, said: "Columbanus is the patron saint of those who seek to construct a united Europe."

It isn't just for their religious impact that the Irish monks are renowned, but for the manner in which they inscribed and illuminated their magnificent manuscripts. "Drawing upon the traditional art of their pagan past, Irish monks decorated their great manuscript books and the accoutrements of their churches with designs that are a breathtaking reminder of the art of their forebears... Margins overflow with patterns of swirling, interlocking lines, and entire pages are given over to scriptural pictures that are a kaleidoscope of colour and restless patterns. Perhaps the most famous of these Bible pages are the dazzling 'carpet pages', covered in their entirety with patterns that rival the delicacy of the finest metalwork and the brilliance of enamel or precious stones."[48] Some of these manuscripts, notably the *Book of Kells*, the *Book of Durrow*, and the *Lindisfarne Gospels*, are considered to be among the world's greatest art treasures.

2 — The Consolidation of Gaelic Ireland

While Irish missionaries were spreading the message of Christianity throughout Europe the Irish at home had not allowed themselves to be deflected from their proclivity for martial conflict.

Around 450, after Emain Macha had been destroyed, or abandoned, as a result of the initial Uí Néill advance, the Ulstermen had retreated east, and in this reduced kingdom of Ulster they attempted to stabilise their power, with the erection of the "Dane's Cast" earthworks as a visible reminder to their adversaries that they were in no respects a spent force.

The Cruthin confronted the Uí Néill in 563 at the battle of Móin Dairi Lothair (Moneymore). However, seven kings of the Cruthin were killed in this battle, and the way was open for the Northern Uí Néill victors to expand into what is now County Londonderry.

In the *Annals of Ulster* the compiler, when giving mention of this battle, also records it in verse:

> Sharp weapons stretch, men stretch,
> In the great bog of Daire-lothair —
> The cause of a contention for right —
> Seven Cruithnian Kings, including Aedh Brec.
> The battle of all the Cruithni is fought,
> [And] they burn Eilne.
> The battle of Gabhair-Lifè is fought,
> And the battle of Cul-dreimne.[35]

Two years later the Cruthin over-king of Ulster, Aed Dub mac Suibni, slew the Northern Uí Néill king, Diarmait mac Cerbaill. A battle is also recorded between the Cruthin and the Uí Néill near Coleraine in 579. However, it was to be at the great battle of Moira in 637 that the Ulstermen were to make their most determined effort to call a halt to Uí Néill expansion.

The Battle of Moira   Congal Cláen, possibly the greatest of all Cruthin kings, became over-king of Ulster in 627. In 628 he slew Suibne Menn, the Uí Néill high-king, but was in turn defeated by the new high-king at Dún Ceithirn in Derry two years later (the battle which Columba's biographer tells us the saint had prophesied to Comgall, the Cruthin abbot of Bangor).

By 637, however, Congal had managed to gather around him a powerful army, which included not only his Ulstermen, but, according to Colgan, contingents of Picts (Scotland), Anglo-Saxons (English) and Britons (Welsh).

The battle, as depicted in later Bardic romances, seems to have been a ferocious affair, and as well as the land confrontation it included a naval engagement.

The *Annals of Tigernach* record the battle as follows:

> AD 637. The Battle of Magh Rath, gained by Domnall, son of Aed, and by the sons of Aed Sláine — but Domnall at this time ruled Temoria — in which fell Congal Caech king of Uladh and Faelan, with many nobles; and in which fell Suibne, son of Colmán Cuar.

In 1872, Sir Samuel Ferguson — born in 1810 and the finest poet of 19th century Ireland — published his masterpiece *Congal*, based on the Bardic romance 'Cath Muighe Rath' (Battle of Moyra). Ferguson's poem is in the grand epic style of the old Irish bards, and it is easy to imagine that this is how they too would have described the mortally wounded king, as he staggered from the battlefield, half-conscious and little knowing what was transpiring around him:

> But, rapt in darkness and in swoon of anguish and despair,
> As in a whirlwind, Congal Cláen seemed borne thro' upper air;
> And, conscious only of the grief surviving at his heart,
> Now deemed himself already dead, and that his deathless part
> Journeyed to judgement; but before what God's or demon's seat
> Dared not conjecture; though, at times, from tramp of giant feet
> And heavy flappings heard in air, around and underneath,
> He darkly surmised who might be the messenger of death
> Who bore him doomward: but anon, laid softly on the ground,
> His mortal body with him still, and still alive he found.

> Loathing the light of day he lay; nor knew nor reck'd he where;
> For present anguish left his mind no room for other care;
> All his great heart to bursting filled with rage, remorse and shame,
> To think what labour come to nought, what hopes of power and fame
> Turned in a moment to contempt; what hatred and disgrace
> Fixed thenceforth irremovably on all his name and race...

> Then Congal raised his drooping head, and saw with bloodshot eyes
> His native vale before him spread; saw grassy Collin rise
> High o'er the homely Antrim hills. He groaned with rage and shame.
> "And have I fled the field," he cried; "and shall my hapless name
> "Become this byword of reproach? Rise; bear me back again,
> "And lay me where I yet may lie among the valiant slain." [49]

In an article reviewing *Reeves' Ecclesiastical Antiquities*, Ferguson, who typified the Ulster intellectual of his day — intensely proud of his 'Gaelic' heritage, but without the rancour of the xenophobe — wrote:

"We are here upon the borders of the heroic field of Moyra, the scene of the greatest battle, whether we regard the numbers engaged, the duration of combat, or the stake at issue, ever fought within the bounds of Ireland. For beyond question, if Congal Cláen and his Gentile allies had been victorious in that battle, the re-establishment of old bardic paganism would have ensued. There appears reason to believe that the fight lasted a week; and on the seventh day Congal himself is said to have been slain by an idiot youth, whom he passed by in battle, in scorn of his imbecility. All local memory of the event is now gone, save that one or two localities preserve names connected with it. Thus, beside the Rath of Moyra, on the east, is the hill Cairn-Albanach, the burial-place of the Scottish princes, Congal's uncles; and a pillar-stone, with a rude cross, and some circles engraved on it, formerly marked the site of their resting-place. On the other hand, the townland of Aughnafoskar probably preserves the name of Knockanchoscar, from which Congal's druid surveyed the royal army, drawn up in the plain below, on the first morning of the battle. Ath Ornav, the ford crossed by one of the armies, is probably modernised in Thorny-ford, on the river, at some miles distance. On the ascent to Trummery, in the direction of the woods of Killultagh, to which, we are told, the routed army fled, great quantities of bones of men and horses were turned up in excavating the line of the Ulster Railway which passes close below the old church." [49]

High-Kingship of Ireland   The story of Congal Cláen has a bearing on another aspect of Irish history — the question of the 'high-kingship' of Ireland. Late seventh century writers claimed that the Uí Néill had held the high-kingship of Ireland for many centuries. Yet in the study of that early period of Irish history little evidence is found of a centralised monarchy. Indeed, at any given time between the fifth and twelfth centuries there were probably no less than 150 tribal kings throughout the island. Francis Byrne has commented: "In later ages this multiplication of monarchies caused some embarrassment to patriotic Irishmen who had been brought up to believe in the glories of the high-kingship centred in Tara... The title *ard-rí*... has no precise significance, and does not necessarily imply sovereignty of Ireland... It is now evident that Niall and his descendants for many centuries can in no real sense be described as high-kings of Ireland. The claims made for them... must be discounted as partisan: few other contemporary documents show special deference being afforded to the Uí Néill outside their own sphere of influence, and the laws do not even envisage the office of high-king of Ireland." [24]

Ironically, the *only* reference to Tara throughout all the Old Irish legal tracts concerns, not a member of the Uí Néill dynasty, but Congal Cláen of the Cruthin. *Bechbretha*, an eighth century law tract, details, among many other matters, how blame should be apportioned for bee stings, stating the following:

> If it be an eye which it has blinded, it is then that it (the injury) requires the casting of lots on all the hives; whichever of the hives it falls upon is forfeit for its (the bee's) offence. For this is the first judgement which was passed with regard to the offences of bees on Congal the One-eyed, whom bees

blinded in one eye. And he was king of Tara until [this] put him from his kingship." [50]

The matter of Congal losing the high-kingship refers to the prohibition on anyone with a blemish holding this position.

As Francis Byrne comments: "This is the only reference in the law-tracts to Tara (and) it runs directly contrary to the accepted doctrine that it was a monopoly of the Uí Néill... When we remember that the Ulaid and Cruthin were still powerful in County Londonderry and possibly still ruled directly in Louth as far as the Boyne in the early seventh century; that they cherished memories of their former dominance over all the North; that they considered the Uí Néill recent upstarts... it is not difficult to imagine that they could with some justice lay claim to Tara." [24]

However, whatever arguments the Ulstermen could have produced to support such a claim were immaterial after 637. The battle of Moira effectively put an end to any hopes they might have harboured that they could undo the Uí Néill gains. For although the Ulstermen were still to retain their independence in the east of the province for another 500 years, the Uí Néill were now firmly entrenched as the dominant power in the North.

Leth Cam and Cráeb Tulcha   As well as their continued victories against the Ulstermen — the Ulaid suffered a severe defeat at Fochairt near Dundalk in 735 — the Uí Néill also continued to encroach upon the territory held by the Airgialla in the centre of the ancient province. It was probably their alarm at this continuing advance which explains why the Ulstermen fought alongside the Airgialla at the battle of Leth Cam (near Armagh) in 827, in which the Uí Néill emerged victorious yet again, with many kings of the Airgialla being slain. Whatever autonomy had been held by the Airgialla was now destroyed and their kings became mere vassals of the Uí Néill.

Despite these reverses, the Ulstermen were still determined to resist, and in 1004 another great battle was fought at Cráeb Tulcha, in which the Cruthin king, the Ulaid king, and many princes of Ulster, were killed — indeed, complete disaster was possibly only averted because the victorious Uí Néill king was also one of the fatalities. The *Annals of Ulster* thus record the event:

> The battle of Craebh-telcha, between the Ulidians and Cinel-Eoghain, where the Ulidians were defeated, and Eochaid, son of Ardgar, King of Ulidia, and Dubhtuinne his brother, and his two sons, viz., Cuduiligh and Domnall, were slain, and a havoc was made of the army besides, between good and bad, viz., Gairbhith, King of Uí-Echach, and Gilla Patraic son of Tomaltach, and Cumuscach son of Flathroe, and Dubhslanga son of Aedh, and Cathalan son of Etroch, and Conene son of Muirchertach, and the elect of the Ulidians besides. And the fighting extended to Dun-Echdach, and to Druim-bó. There also fell there Aedh, son of Domnall Ua Neill, King of

Ailech, (and others, in the 29th year of his age, and the 10th year of [his] reign). But the Cinel-Eoghain say that he was killed by themselves. Donnchad Ua Loingsigh, King of Dal nAraidi, was treacherously killed by the Cinel-Eoghain.[35]

Dynastic Profusion No doubt many of the original peoples of Ulster remained in the territories now dominated by the Uí Néill overlords, but their former dynastic leaders from within the Cruthin and the Ulaid were confined to that area which today comprises counties Antrim, Down and north Louth. Yet, so long as these Ulster kingships endured, no matter how reduced might be the realm over which their suzerainty could lay claim, the Uí Néill could never call themselves kings of Ulster. Cruthin and Ulaid kings shared in the high-kingship of this reduced Ulster, though at times the strains within the alliance would lead to open warfare (it was a battle between the Cruthin and Ulaid, recorded in the *Annals of Ulster* as having been fought at the 'Fearsat' in 667 which gave Belfast its first mention in history). The independent territories became known by the names of the ruling dynasties, prefixed by the term in Gaelic for 'a portion' —'Dál' (Gaelic by now being the dominant language throughout Ireland).

Within the Ulaid the dominant dynasty were the Dál Fiatach, who ruled over the maritime areas between Dundrum Bay and Belfast Lough, with the centre of their power established at Downpatrick. Another grouping, the Dál Riata, held territory in the north-eastern part of Antrim, called Dalriada.

It was, however, the Cruthin who formed the bulk of the population, and their territories comprised the remainder of the area of Antrim and Down, although for some time after the initial Uí Néill advances they had managed to retain their hold on territory northwards to Lough Foyle and southwards to Dundalk Bay. There is evidence of the existence of from seven to nine petty kingdoms of the Cruthin around the sixth century. Their main dynasty was the Dál nAraidi, and the area they ruled over became known in English as Dalaradia (not to be confused with Dalriada in the north-east). The kings of Dál nAraidi resided at Ráth Mor, where a ringfort remains to this day, just east of Antrim town. Another group within the Cruthin who also provided over-kings of Ulster were the Uí Echach Cobo, who inhabited the present baronies of Upper and Lower Iveagh and Kinelarty.

Establishing a Pedigree When the Gaelic dynasties became indisputably into their ascendancy, their learned men sought to provide them with a lineage that would glorify their remarkable achievements. Furthermore, the Gaels had not only imposed their military control over much of Ireland, but, perhaps due to their great influence, prestige and positions of 'political' power, their language had now become widely accepted among the Irish population, certainly among the learned classes and within the developing Church. No doubt the mass of the population for a long time retained much of

42

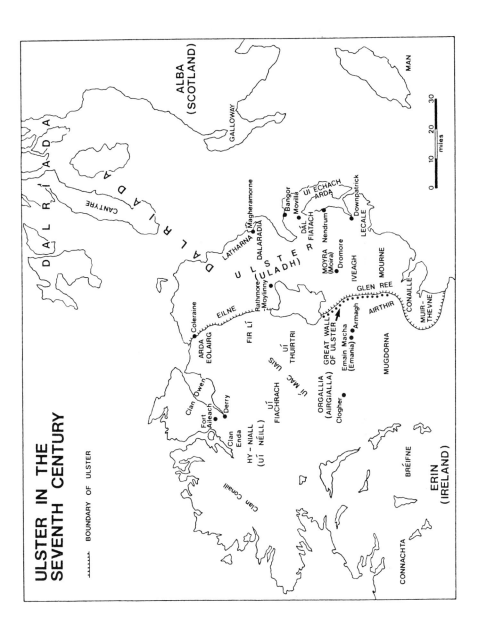

ULSTER IN THE
SEVENTH CENTURY

- - - - - BOUNDARY OF ULSTER

ALBA
(SCOTLAND)

MAN

GALLOWAY

D A L R I A D A

CANTYRE

D A L R I A D A

LATHARNA

Magheramorne

Rathmore
-Moylinny
DALARADIA

Bangor
Movilla

UÍ ECHACH
ARDA

DÁL
FIATACH

Downpatrick

EILNE

Coleraine

U L S T E R
(ULADH)

Nendrum

LECALE

MOYRA
(Moira)

Dromore

IVEAGH

MOURNE

ARDA
EOLAIRG

FIR LÍ

GLEN REE

Clan Owen

UÍ
THUIRTRI

GREAT WALL
OF ULSTER

AIRTHIR

CONAILLE

Derry

Fort
Aileach

UÍ MAC UAIS

Emain Macha
(Emania)

Armagh

MUIR-
THEVNE

Clan
Enda

UÍ
FIACHRACH

ORGALLIA
(AIRGIALLA)

MUGDORNA

HY - NIALL
(UÍ NÉILL)

Clogher

Clan Conaill

BRÉIFNE

CONNACHTA

ERIN
(IRELAND)

0   10   20   30
miles

43

their own language or languages — references in ancient texts indicate this was so — but these languages must inevitably have gone into decline, although with many loan-words being incorporated into the new 'Irish' language.

The clergy, who had been to the forefront of the development of writing, had originally used Latin, but eventually it was they who were to give the lead to the creative flowering of vernacular Irish literature. The clergy did not limit their efforts just to religious topics, but to the transformation of the wealth of oral tradition into a remarkably rich body of secular literature. And, of course, to the construction of 'genealogies' which would establish suitable pedigrees for the ruling classes.

That the dominant classes desired to see themselves thus promoted should hardly surprise us — most ruling establishments throughout history have always sought to see their credentials well established, not just for the pragmatic political needs of the moment but often with an eye to posterity. And so the Gaelic genealogists set to their task with an energy and inventiveness which even today provokes admiration from scholars.

One of the main works produced as a result of this intensive effort was the *Lebor Gabála*, the 'Book of Invasions', which sought to enumerate all the successive invasions of Ireland and all the peoples who partook in those invasions. Leaving aside its genealogical purpose, the account stands by itself as a fascinating collection of legends, within which stalk mysterious peoples and their powerful heroes, constantly fighting gigantic battles — and which can still today provide a rich source of inspiration, as is witnessed by the beautifully imaginative illustrations of Irish artist Jim Fitzpatrick.

Within this account the ancestors of the Gaels are said to have sprung from two sons of Míl, a warrior who had come to Ireland from Spain. In the earliest version (eighth century) only a limited number of ethnic groupings are awarded this important pedigree, while all others are relegated to an inferior status. Then, in a later, 'revised edition' of *Lebor Gabála*, Míl seems to have posthumously increased his sons, for a third, Ir, is now present. As T.F. O'Rahilly commented: "The invention of Ir was probably due in the first instance to the genealogists, who were favourably disposed towards the Cruthin and determined to provide them with a highly respectable Goidelic [Gaelic] pedigree."[51]

This process continued, with other important Irish dynasties being incorporated into the Milesian family tree, the number of Míl's sons eventually increasing to eight. However, as Francis Byrne pointed out, "the mythological material is so rich and varied that not even the most assiduous monkish synchroniser nor the most diplomatic fabricator of pedigrees could bring complete order into this chaos. The resultant inconsistencies and anachronisms give us valuable clues."[24]

T. F. O'Rahilly, in his monumental work *Early Irish History and Mythology*, tried to reassemble the jigsaw of early Irish origins, although his conclusions as to *who* the various peoples in *Lebor Gabála* might have been are questioned today. Nevertheless, O'Rahilly neatly summed up the process by which the

Gaelic genealogists undertook their task:

"In the early Christian centuries the ethnic origins of the different sections of the Irish population were vividly remembered, so much so that one of the chief aims of the early Irish historians and genealogists, was to efface these distinctions from the popular memory. This they did by inventing for the Irish people generally (apart from the lower classes, who did not count) a common ancestor in the fictitious Míl of Spain... The 'learned' authors of that elaborate fiction, the invasion of the Sons of Míl, and the genealogy-makers who collaborated with them, were animated by the desire to invest the Goidelic occupation of Ireland with an antiquity to which it was entitled neither in fact nor in tradition; for only in this way would it be feasible to provide a Goidelic descent for tribes of non-Goidelic origin, and to unify the divergent ethnic elements in the country by tracing them back to a common ancestor... [By] obliterating the memory of the different ethnic origins of the people... the tribes of pre-Celtic descent were turned officially into Goidels... It was necessary to discountenance the popular view that the Goidels were, comparatively speaking, late-comers to this country, and so the authors boldly and deliberately pushed back the Goidelic invasion into the remote past." [51]

This re-writing of history was eventually to have its desired result, as O'Rahilly noted with particular reference to the Cruthin:

"The Cruthin or Priteni are the earliest inhabitants of these islands to whom a name can be assigned... The combined influence of Bede, Mael Mura, and the genealogical fiction of Ir, caused *Cruithni* to lose favour as the name of a section of the Irish population. This disuse of *Cruithni* as a name is doubtless connected with the rise of a new genealogical doctrine which turned the Irish Cruthin into Goidels and thus disassociated them from the Cruthin of Scotland. Nevertheless the fact that there were Cruthin in Ireland as well as in Scotland was, as might be expected, long remembered; and so it is not surprising to find writers occasionally suggesting, in defiance of Mael Mura, that the Cruthin of both countries formed one people in remote times."

3 — The Scottish Connection

It is to this 'Scottish connection' that we shall now turn. We have already seen that the link between Ireland and Scotland goes back to when man first established himself in Ireland, one substantial piece of evidence being the appearance in both north-east Ireland and south-west Scotland of an identical type of megalithic grave — which have been labelled the 'Clyde-Carlingford cairns' by archaeologists to highlight the definite link across the North Channel.

While the ease of accessibility provided by the narrow waters of the North Channel would lead us to suppose that commerce and movement between the two areas was of a regular and extensive nature, it is only as we approach the 'historical' age that documentary evidence is provided for such intercourse.

Argyll   Possibly because of the pressure of the Uí Néill territorial gains, and the contraction of Old Ulster, groups within the Northern population began to move across the North Channel, in particular the Dál Riata, who settled Argyll and the islands along the western seaboard. The Venerable Bede, writing in the 8th century (*A History of the English Church and People*), states that this land was obtained from the local Pictish people by a combination of force and treaty. The kings of the Dál Riata soon claimed sovereignty over territory on both sides of the North Channel, and when Fergus MacErc forsook his Irish capital of Dunseverick around 500 and established his main residence in Argyll, we may assume that by this time the colony had ousted the mother-country in importance. After their defeat alongside Congal Cláen at the great battle of Moira in 637, however, the Dalriadan kings were finally to lose their Ulster territories to the Uí Néill.

Groups from Ireland had been raiding Roman Britain, according to Roman writers, as early as 343. To the Romans the Irish raiders were called 'Scotti', and Ireland became known as Scotia. However, while Ireland was eventually to lose that appellation, the new settlers crossing the North Channel were to bequeath the name to their new homeland. From the kings of Dalriada there is a direct link to the kings of what would become 'Scotland'.

Galloway   The settlement of northern Irish in Argyll has tended to overshadow a later movement across the North Channel — that of a migration of Cruthin to Galloway. As Charles Thomas wrote: "An admirable guide to the early Irish settlement could be constructed from the distribution of certain place-name elements — particularly those relating to simple natural features. [Such names are found in] an intense localized concentration in the double peninsula of the Rhinns of Galloway, opposite Antrim. No special historical sources describe what now looks like another early Irish colony here — possibly of the sixth century. But isolated archaeological finds from Galloway, the spread of a type of early ecclesiastical site (the enclosed developed cemetery) which may be regarded as Irish-inspired, and several minor pointers in the same direction, are mounting to reliable evidence for a separate settlement in this south-western area." [52]

The church at Bangor would have had strong links with this area, indeed a Bangor monk became Abbot of St Ninian's old monastery of Candida Casa at the end of the sixth century. Churches in Galloway were often dedicated to saints popular in Ulster. Chalmers dated the main Cruthinic movements to the Galloway region to the eighth century "followed by fresh swarms from the Irish hive in the ninth and tenth centuries." [53]

Such a settlement by Ulster Cruthin may help to explain the references in old texts (Reginald of Durham, Jocelyn of Furness and Richard of Hexham) to the 'Picts of Galloway'. Such references had troubled some historians, for the Scottish Picts were not believed to have dwelt so far south of the Antonine Wall, erected by the Romans to keep them at bay. However, the place-name and archaeological evidence indicating the link with Ulster provides an answer to the problem. Furthermore, the old Welsh records speak of the people of this area as *Gwyddel Ffichti* or 'Irish Picts'.

Scots/Irish
Culture Province
These settlers had already absorbed the Gaelic language while in Ulster, and they were to carry it with them to Scotland. This new language, over the succeeding centuries, was eventually to spread throughout Scotland. The ancient traditions of Ulster which the settlers brought with them remained strong among the ordinary people long after they had disappeared from many parts of Ireland. Evidence of pre-Celtic and Celtic customs also abound throughout the Scottish-Irish 'culture province' and much Ulster Folk material could still be collected in the Highlands and Islands of Scotland well into the 20th century.

With the arrival of the Christian period and the intensive missionary activity that spread to Scotland, initiated by men of vision and energy such as Comgall and Columba, the cross-fertilisation between Scotland and Ulster was to reach new heights, particularly in respect to the flowering of literary creativeness. As Proinsias Mac Cana wrote:

"Isolation tends towards stagnation, or at least a circumscribed vision, while conversely intercourse and cultural commerce encourage a greater intellectual curiosity and awareness, a greater readiness to adapt old ways and experiment with new ones. For such intercourse the east-Ulster region was ideally situated. It was a normal landing-place for travellers from northern Britain, which during the sixth and seventh centuries probably presented a more dramatic clash and confluence of cultures than any other part of Britain or Ireland; and, in addition, the religious, social and political ties that linked north-eastern Ireland and north-western Britain — particularly in that period — were numerous and close. Archaeologists speak of an 'Irish Sea culture-province' with its western flank in Ireland and its eastern flank in Britain; one might with comparable justification speak of a North Channel culture-province within which obtained a free currency of ideas, literary, intellectual and artistic.

"One recalls particularly those tales which relate in one way or another to the commerce that existed between east-Ulster and Scotland: for instance, the story of Suibne Geilt, whom the later evolution of his legend makes king of Dál Riata—by James Carney's reasoning it must have passed from Scotland to Ireland before c.800; or the several thematically related tales which make up what one might call the 'Tristan complex' and which also link Irish and north British tradition." [40]

Cruthin
and Pict
The ancient inhabitants of the British Isles had been known to the Greeks as the 'Pretani'. Later 'Pretani' became 'Cruthin' and when medieval Irish writers referred to these people it is clear they considered them to inhabit both Ireland and Scotland. One writer stated that 'thirty kings of the Cruthin ruled Ireland and Scotland from Ollam to Fiachna

mac Baetáin,' and that 'seven kings of the Cruthin of Scotland ruled Ireland in Tara ' (*secht rig do Chruithnibh Alban rofhallnastair Erind i Temair*) — thereby identifying, as T.F. O'Rahilly notes, "the Cruthin of Ireland with those of Scotland". [51] Others refer to Scotland as the 'land of the Cruthin', while in a poem written in the eleventh or twelfth century the author tells us that the *Cruthnig* made up a section of the population of Scotland. The Annals of Tigernach, The Pictish Chronicle, St Berchan, the Albanic Duan, the Book of Deer and John of Fordun plainly show that the name Cruthin was applied to the inhabitants of both Scotland and Ireland.

The word 'Pretani' is also the forerunner of the Welsh *Prydyn*, which means primarily 'Picts' and secondarily 'Pictland'. Eventually, the Pretanic people of Scotland were to be more generally labelled Picts, though the Pretani of Ireland were never given this appellation by those writing in Latin (more modern writers, however, have quite freely interchanged the terms 'Irish Pict' and 'Cruthin'). The Picts of Scotland did not disappear from history: as Liam de Paor points out: "The Picts undoubtedly contributed much to the make-up of the medieval kingdom of Scotland, forming probably the bulk of its population." [54]

Because the ancient Irish considered the older inhabitants of Scotland and the northern part of Ireland to be from the same ethnic stock, it would be fascinating to know just how close that kinship was. Certainly, many factors lend weight to the probability that it was very close. For a start, the geographical proximity of Scotland and Ulster would certainly facilitate the same people establishing themselves on both sides of the North Channel. Scholars also acknowledge that the older population groups of Europe, if they survived reasonably intact at all under the impact of the Indo-European invasions, would have done so mainly at the peripheral fringes of the Continent, such as Ireland and Scotand. Further, archaeologists now believe that the inhabitants of the 'Highland zone' of the British Isles — which includes Ireland and Scotland — are primarily of pre-Celtic stock. There are even indications of language similarities — when St Columba went to Scotland to try and convert the King of the Picts, he took with him St Comgall, the Cruthin abbot of Bangor, and St Canice, "who, being Irish Picts, were the better able to confer with the Picts [of Scotland]." [42] So, even if the archaeological and historical evidence may not as yet allow us to establish the exact extent of the kinship between the pre-Celtic peoples of Scotland and Ulster, there is at the same time nothing that necessarily contradicts the assertion of the ancient writers themselves that "the Cruthin of both areas formed one people in remote times."

As Liam de Paor commented: "The gene pool of the Irish... is probably very closely related to the gene pools of highland Britain... Within that fringe area, relationships, both cultural and genetic, almost certainly go back to a much more distant time than that uncertain period when Celtic languages and customs came to dominate both Great Britain and Ireland. Therefore, so far as the physical make-up of the Irish goes... they share these origins with their fellows

48

in the neighbouring parts — the north and west — of the next-door island of Great Britain." [55]

Just as the 'Cruthin' of Scotland eventually became known as Picts, so in Ireland, as we have already seen, the name Cruthin also fell into disuse, to be replaced by the names of their dynastic households. Yet, in 784 the *Annals of Ulster* recorded the death of Coisenech 'nepos Predeni', King of the Iveagh Cruthin. The existence of this pre-Gaelic name, Predeni (Pretani), so late in Irish history is astonishing, and shows how tenacious the Cruthin were to the memories of their former greatness.

4 — New Invaders

The Vikings In 793, the Danes attacked the Anglican monastery of Lindisfarne on the east coast of Britain, while on the west the Norse sacked the monastery of Iona in 795. In 811 the Ulaid clashed with the Norse Vikings and defeated them. In 823 the Norse pillaged Bangor monastery, in a devastating assault during which it is said that 3,000 people died, manuscripts were destroyed and the monastery utterly wrecked. In 825 they raided Downpatrick and Movilla, but were eventually badly beaten by the Ulaid in Leth Cathail (Lecale).

These repeated attacks occasionally met with concerted resistance. In 912, despite having been recently engaged in battle against one another, the Ulaid King, Hugh, and Niall Glundubh of the Uí Néill, agreed to a peace treaty which was ratified at Tullyhogue in Tyrone. The result was that, when Niall waged war on the Norse, the Ulaid were in support, and both kings fell together at the battle of Dublin in 919.

Yet despite the threat posed by these Scandinavian incursions, the internecine warring among the Irish continued as before, and the newcomers were inevitably drawn in. In 933 Matudan mac Hugh of the Ulaid raided Monaghan with Norse allies but was routed by the Uí Néill (Matudan is commemorated in Ben Madigan, now Cave Hill, overlooking Belfast). In 942 the Norse raided Downpatrick, but were defeated after a pursuit by the Ulaid. The following year the Ulaid of Lecale exterminated the Norse of Strangford Lough. In 949 Matudan made the fatal mistake of plundering the Cruthin of Conailli Muirthemne in Louth. The affront was avenged by the Iveagh Cruthin when they slew Matudan a year later.

The early raiding of these Scandinavian invaders gave way to the establishment of permanent settlements, the development of trade and commerce, and the founding of such centres as Dublin, Wexford, Waterford, Wicklow, Cork and Limerick.

Despite this important contribution to Irish society, the Viking period is still regarded in the popular imagination as one of depredation and pillage. As Estyn Evans commented: "However much historians differ, there has been a tacit understanding that the Celtic invasion was somehow 'good'... We have no record of what the natives thought about it. The Viking invasion on the other hand was 'bad': it came late enough for its misdeeds to be documented." [10]

Yet, if we consider the burning and pillaging of churches attributed to the Vikings by early Irish propagandists, it has been asserted that at least half of these, from the 7th century to the 16th, were perpetrated by the Irish themselves, not only before the Vikings came, but long after the Scandinavians were absorbed into Irish society. [56]

The Anglo- At the battle of Hastings in 1066, William, Duke of Normandy,
Normans a descendant of Norse settlers in France, defeated the Anglo-
Saxons and commenced the Norman conquest of England. It would not be long before these Normans set foot in Ireland, though, ironically, not by 'invasion', but by 'invitation'.

Another irony, as Lewis Warren points out, is that, despite the dramatic effect these new arrivals were to have on Irish history, "The English suffered more from the Normans than the Irish ever did. In Domesday Book there is no trace of the great families which had ruled England before 1066; in Ireland the leading families whose names are familiar from long before the Normans arrived are still there four hundred years later." [57]

In 1169 the first 'Anglo-Normans' arrived on Irish soil, at the request of Dermot Mac Murchada, deposed King of Leinster, who sought their aid in a bid to regain his kingship. The first to arrive were Norman knights like Fitzstephen and then Fitzgerald, and eventually families such as these would become 'more Irish than the Irish'. The main contingent arrived with Strongbow (Richard de Clare, Earl of Pembroke) on 23 August 1170 at Waterford. Although these new arrivals are generally termed 'Anglo-Norman', it should be remembered that the Norman conquest of England and Wales was a relatively recent one. There the Norman French had many Old British (Brêtons) among them whose heritage was similar to the Welsh among whom they settled, and was expressed romantically in the Arthurian Chronicles. In actuality, therefore, Strongbow's force was a Cambro-Norman one, and far from 'English' in either culture, language or composition.

English Henry II was concerned with the growing independence of
Intervention his supposed followers in Ireland. He arrived in Ireland to
set matters straight, making his barons swear loyalty and then parcelling out the country between them and the Irish chieftains. As Lewis Warren commented: "Henry II had no intention of conquering Ireland; he wanted to stop the Normans doing it. He made a treaty with the High King by which he was to have charge of the Normans and Rory [O'Connor, king of Connaught] was to mind the Irish... Significantly he never included Ireland among his lordships. He was king of England, duke of Normandy, count of Anjou and duke of Aquitaine. That is how he styled himself: Ireland was not a welcome acquisition; it was a nuisance." [57]

The Earldom of Ulster   In 1177 one of the baronial adventurers, John de Courcy, marched north and captured Downpatrick. What the Gaelic chieftains had begun but not completed — the final end to Ulster's independence — was now to be accomplished by de Courcy, who made himself 'Master of Ulster' (princeps Ultoniae). Although he owed fealty to Henry II of England, this title was purely of de Courcy's own making. The Ulidian king, Mac Donleavy, still officially remained 'Rex Ulidiae'. De Courcy's greatest achievements were the establishment of towns and ports and the building of two fine castles, at Carrickfergus and Dundrum. At first strongly opposed by the Ulstermen, de Courcy's government was soon seen by them to offer some degree of protection against continuing attacks by the O'Neills. In 1181 the Clan Owen "gained a battle over the Ulidians, and over Uí Tuirtri, and over Fir-Li around Rory Mac Donleavy and Cumee O'Flynn." Increasing raids by the Clan Owen in which they "took many thousands of cows" forced the Ulidians to appeal to de Courcy for help. And so, when the Devlins and their kin made their next raid in 1182, they were met and defeated by de Courcy in alliance with the Ulidians.

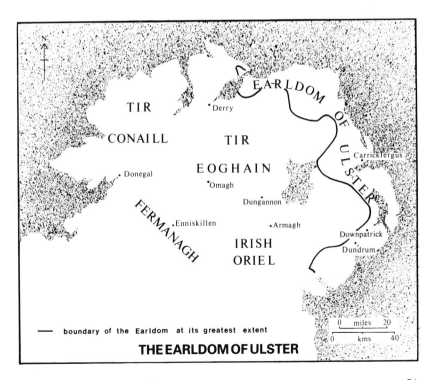

boundary of the Earldom at its greatest extent

THE EARLDOM OF ULSTER

De Courcy's independent rule in Ulster now aroused the jealousy of Hugh de Lacy, who misrepresented the Master of Ulster to the new King John of England. Following this de Courcy fell into disfavour, and was defeated by de Lacy at Downpatrick. Finally, on 29 May, 1205, King John granted de Lacy all of de Courcy's lands, and created him Earl of Ulster. De Lacy and his half-brother Walter soon showed John that he had mistaken his men, for by 1208 they were at war with 'the English of Munster', and proved more insubordinate than the Irish themselves.

Gaelic Resistance   Although the Gaelic chiefs continued to resist the Anglo-Norman presence, this did not inhibit constant warfare between the O'Donnells of Tirconnell and the O'Neills of Tirowen. In 1258 a conference was held to promote a spirit of unity among the Gaelic chiefs. At this gathering Brian O'Neill was elected 'high-king', although important figures such as Donald Oge O'Donnell refused to acknowledge him. One result, however, was the forging of an alliance between Brian O'Neill and Felim O'Connor, King of Connacht. This alliance was crushed by the 'English' at the battle of Downpatrick in 1260. The Iveagh Cruthin and the Ulaid refused to join the O'Neills at this battle, a confirmation perhaps that in Ireland deep-seated antagonism to old enemies can last a very long time.

As the Anglo-Norman expansion continued, the O'Neills still coveted each other's property. In 1275 the Tirowen (Tyrone) families invaded Tirconnell and devastated the entire district. Following this incursion they were pursued by O'Donnell of Tirconnell and defeated "with the loss of men, horses, accoutrements, arms and armour." In 1283 the positions were reversed, and it was the turn of Tirconnell to be heavily defeated by O'Neill of Tirowen. The 'English' of the north were now led by Richard de Burgh, the 'Red Earl of Ulster'. Richard's father Walter had inherited the de Lacy territory by right of his wife, who was Hugh de Lacy's daughter. So, in 1286, we find Richard compelling the submission of the O'Donnell. He also deposed the O'Neill of Tyrone for a time, and in 1290 again plundered Tirconnell. Later he planted a colony in Inishowen and erected a castle at Moville to command the whole district.

The Scottish Invasion   On 24 June 1314 the Scots, under Robert the Bruce, defeated the English at the battle of Bannockburn. The natural extension of the victory of Scottish independence was the invitation of O'Neill of Tyrone to Robert offering to make his brother Edward — then 'Lord of Galloway' — King of Ireland. Robert accepted readily for the fierce ambition of his brother was a threat to the King of Scots himself. And so, on 25 May, 1315, Edward Bruce landed at Larne Harbour on the Antrim coast. He was joined by Robert Bissett with the Scots of Antrim and by Donald O'Neill son of Brian of Tyrone.

In response to this threat, and in spite of his age, Richard, the Red Earl of

Ulster, assembled his retainers in Roscommon and marched to Athlone, where he was joined by Felim O'Connor and the army of Connacht. This 'English' army then marched into Ulster, laying waste the country of the O'Neill.

Meanwhile Bruce had overrun Down and Louth, devastating old Ulster, destroying the 'English' there and their Ulidian support. Then, according to the *Annals of Clonmacnoise* "by the procurement of O'Neale and Ulstermen he took his journey to Cowllerayne (Coleraine) of the North and to the borders of Innisowen, and fell down and broke the bridge of Cowllerayne to stop the Earl's passage over the river of Bann, whom the Earl followed until he came to the same river, and from thence thro' Ulster, where he marched holding on their course of spoyleing and destroying all places where they came."

Both armies then faced each other across the troubled waters of the bridgeless Bann. At this point O'Connor deserted the Red Earl, who was thus forced to retreat and subsequently defeated in battle near Ballymena on 10 September, 1315. Following a campaign of devastation Edward was eventually crowned King of Ireland on 1 May, 1316, in the presence of a large assembly of Irish and Scottish nobles. Edward was finally defeated by an 'English' force under John de Birmingham at Faughart near Dundalk in 1318. Edward was killed in this battle and with the death of this cruelly ambitious but exceptionally brave Lord of Galloway, the Scottish invasion came to an end.

Edward Bruce had brought with him some 6,000 Scottish mercenaries, called 'galloglasses', and over the next few centuries it was to these Scots, many of whom settled here, that much of the resurgence of Gaelic Ireland can be attributed.

Extinction of Ancient Ulaid   However, the power of the Earls of Ulster was crushed. The devastation in Ulster was followed by famine and famine was followed by disease. All over Ulster the Anglo-Normans Gaelicised themselves to survive; the de Burghs adopted the name Burke, the de Mandevilles became the McQuillans, Lords of the Route (Dalriata). Only in Dublin and its 'Pale' did the 'English' government keep control.

With the destruction of the Anglo-Normans in the North the O'Neills now began to claim the whole of Ulster. Up to now, as T.E. McNeill points out, they had been "forced constantly to admit that they had no right to it in English or Irish law... For over 500 years it had been well known that Navan belonged to the Ulaid [and] the Uí Néill dynasties had no claim to Ulster in the traditional sense." [58] Despite this, a branch of the Uí Néill dynasty, known as the O'Neills of Clandeboye, planted themselves upon the ruins of the Earldom of Ulster. It was not until 1364, however, that Aedh Mór Ua Neill was styled 'king of Ulster' by the *Annals of Ulster*, and it was only in 1381 that Niall Ua Néill could legitimize his claim to Ulster in the eyes of the learned classes when he held a great feast for them near Emain Macha. As Francis Byrne pointed out: "The restoration of the name Ulster to cover once again the whole North was made possible only by the extinction of the kingdom of Ulaid." [24]

Modern

1381 — present

1 — Conquest, Resistance and Plantation

Elizabethan Effective English control had eventually become confined to
Re-conquest Dublin and to an ever-shrinking area around it known as 'the
Pale'. Not only were the Irish chiefs beyond royal jurisdiction
but many of the first Anglo-Norman settlers had become so assimilated into
Irish life — indeed, becoming 'more Irish than the Irish' — that their loyalty
was increasingly suspect. Henry VIII's daughter, Elizabeth I, however, set out
to rectify this unacceptable state of affairs. As Robert Kee pointed out: "Her
deputies in Ireland were Englishmen newly appointed from England, and no
longer those old Norman-English Irish lords who had so often proved to be
simply their own masters in the past. Force 'when necessity requireth' was
applied equally against the Old English and the Gaelic Irish, with unprecedented
savagery." [59]

Irish opposition to this new stage of the English 'conquest' was strongest in
Ulster. The two ruling clans, the O'Neills and O'Donnells, were involved in a
serious rebellion from 1594 to 1601. In 1594 Hugh O'Donnell opened the
rebellion by defeating an English army at the 'Ford of the Biscuits', with
O'Neill joining him the following year. In May 1595 Sir Henry Bagenal, on
his way back from relieving the English outpost of Monaghan, was ambushed
at Clontibret and suffered heavy losses. In 1598 O'Neill and O'Donnell
dramatically defeated Bagenal at the Yellow Ford, to the south of Lough
Neagh. This defeat, which inspired risings in other parts of Ireland, shook the
new English government to its foundations.

The English recovered and in 1601 under Mountjoy they finally broke the
Gaelic rebellion at Kinsale, after O'Neill had been forced to leave his familiar
Ulster territory to link up with a Spanish force which had landed in the south of
Ireland.

'Flight of On 4 September, 1607, after continued harassment by Crown
the Earls' officials, many of Ulster's Gaelic chieftains, including the Earls
of Tyrone and Tirconnell, chose voluntary exile and sailed from
Rathmullan for Europe. This 'Flight of the Earls' gave the English government
the opportunity to declare their lands forfeit, and some 750,000 acres were
confiscated by the Crown.

When the Ulster chieftains fought against the English they were not fighting
'for Ireland' in the modern nationalist sense but in their own interests and to
preserve their ancient Gaelic way of life. The very idea of a republican form of
government would have been repugnant to the old Irish system of law. In his
Life of Hugh O'Neill (1845) the Young Irelander John Mitchel pointed out
that: "Furthermore there was, in the 16th century, no Irish nation. Save the tie
of a common language, the chieftain of Clan Connal (O'Donnell) had no more
connection with the Lord of Clan Carrha (Cork), than either one had with the

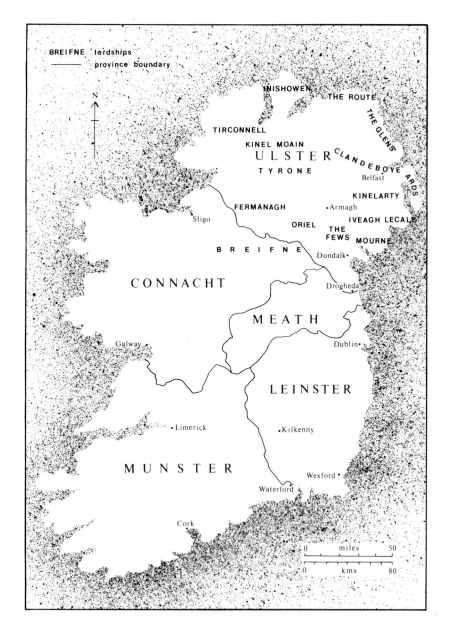

ANGLO-IRISH AND GAELIC LORDSHIPS IN THE LATE 15TH CENTURY

English Pale. The Anglo-Norman colony was regarded as one of the independent tribes of the island."

It was at this time that a new provincial configuration of Ireland was effected with four 'provinces' divided up into counties. The eastern part of the Kingdom of Breffny (Cavan) was taken from Connaught and placed artificially in Ulster while the northern part of Louth, which had been one of the most ancient parts of Ulster, known originally as Muirtheimne and defended by the legendary hero Cúchulainn, was taken from Ulster and placed artificially into Leinster. The older boundaries were, however, remembered well into the 17th century. It is ironic that today staunch Irish nationalists have lost sight of that ancient demarcation, and instead speak of the new configuration drawn up by the Queen of England's administrators as if it had existed from time immemorial.

The Plantation　The ravages of the cruel and bloody war fought by the Elizabethan English against O'Neill left large areas of Ulster virtually without inhabitants. As well as that, the Crown now controlled the vast territory confiscated following the 'Flight of the Earls'. King James I decided to plant settlers in Ulster, hoping that at the very least it might prove a way of 'civilising' this most rebellious part of Ireland once and for all.

In 1610, Sir Arthur Chichester was to be "the chief architect of the Plantation in Ulster".[60] Yet, he was not completely happy with his task. He complained that while good English settlers were being sent to the territories now opening up in the new land of America, most of those coming to Ulster were to be Scots. Chichester, who bore no real affection for the Irish, thought no more favourably towards the Scots. "He had no special affection for Scotsmen, high or low, gentle or simple, and besides he had spent much of his time and ingenuity ever since his coming to Ireland, in the work of repelling and expelling Islesmen and other Northern Scots from the coasts of Ulster." [61]

Chichester could have saved himself much wasted effort in his attempts to 'repel' such immigrants from across the North Channel if he had realised just how much coming and going there had been between Ulster and Scotland throughout history. As P.L. Henry pointed out: "The mould was fixed in ancient times and modern developments continue ancient associations. We need but think of the Pictish Kingdoms in both areas, of the Ulster-Scottish Kingdom of Dalriada from the last quarter of the 5th to the close of the 8th century, of the Scottish Kingdom founded under Gaelic leadership in 842, of Irish relations with the Kingdom of the Hebrides and Argyll from the 12th century, particularly the immigration of Hebridean soldiers (gallowglasses) from the 13th to the 16th century. There was a constant coming and going between North East Ireland and Western Scotland. The Glens of Antrim were in the hands of Scottish Macdonalds by 1400, and for the next two hundred years Gaelic-speaking Scots came in large numbers. The 17th century immigration of a numerous Scots element need not be considered outside the preceding series." [62]

Many of these Scots, particularly those who came from areas in Scotland which in previous centuries had been populated by immigrants from Ulster, may be justly considered as returning to the home of their ancestors. Thus F.J. Bigger has written that "When the Galloway planters came to Ulster they were only returning to their own lands like emigrants returning home again." [63] These common origins were well known to the settlers themselves as the speech made by Sir James Hamilton in the Irish House of Commons on 1 May 1615 clearly demonstrates.

However, there was to be one fundamental characteristic which would stamp these new arrivals as different from all those who had preceded them — the Reformation had swept Scotland and most of the new arrivals were to be Protestants.

The Reformation   The Reformation in Scotland had brought a social as well as a religious transformation. The development of a strong peasant movement against the feudal lords was expressed politically in democratic ideals as well as culturally in the form of Presbyterianism. When these Lowland Scots came to Ulster they were determined to leave feudalism behind them in Scotland. The new settlers rapidly transformed the Ulster countryside, draining in particular the drumlin country which had stood as a barrier to communication between Ulster and the rest of Ireland since prehistoric times. In extending the Scottish Lowland way of life into Ulster they were soon to see themselves as founders of a new society based on the fundamental rights of liberty, equality and fraternity.

It is wrong to assume, however, that all the settlers were Protestants, since there were Scottish Catholics as well, some of whom were ultimately of English origin. Thus a letter written by the Bishop of Derry to the Lord Chancellor in the year 1692 says, "Sir George Hamilton since he got part of the Earl of Abercorn's grant of the Barony of Strabane has done his best to plant Popery there, and has brought over priests and Jesuits from Scotland." It further laments that "all the Hamilton lands are now in the hands of Papists". A. Perceval-Maxwell has confirmed that, since both Abercorn's and Sir Claud Hamilton's children were converted to Roman Catholicism through Sir George's influence, within a generation one of the most successful parts of the Scottish Plantation was led by Roman Catholics. Most other immigrants were probably at least nominally Protestant although initially their religious affiliations were not strong and the development of their ideals took place in Ulster itself, depending more on local religious leaders than on previous sentiment. [64]

The new Scots settlers differed from the English in language on two counts. Firstly there was a significant group who spoke Gaelic and it seems that Scottish Gaelic speakers were intelligible to the Irish at this period. (Indeed, the first book ever to be printed in Irish Gaelic was a translation of the Calvinist *Book of Common Order*, commonly called John Knox's Liturgy, published in Edinburgh in 1567 for the use of Presbyterians.) Secondly, the

SEVENTEENTH CENTURY SETTLEMENTS IN ULSTER

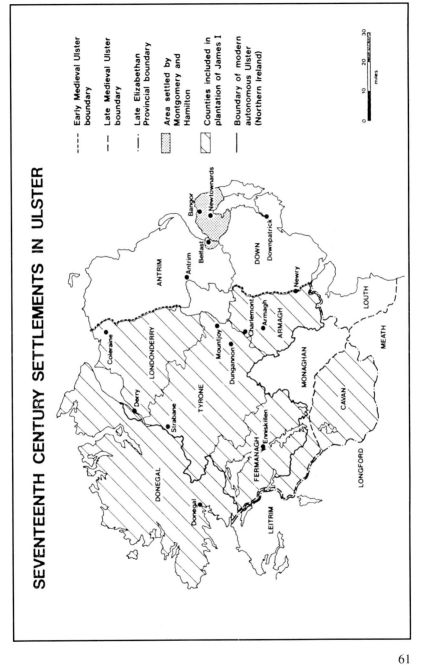

Early Medieval Ulster boundary

Late Medieval Ulster boundary

Late Elizabethan Provincial boundary

Area settled by Montgomery and Hamilton

Counties included in plantation of James I

Boundary of modern autonomous Ulster (Northern Ireland)

miles

0   10   20   30

DONEGAL

LONDONDERRY

Coleraine

Derry

Strabane

TYRONE

Mountjoy

Dungannon

FERMANAGH

Enniskillen

LEITRIM

CAVAN

MONAGHAN

ARMAGH

Charlemont

Armagh

Newry

ANTRIM

Antrim

Belfast

Bangor

Newtownards

DOWN

Downpatrick

LONGFORD

MEATH

LOUTH

language of the others was not the standard English of today but Lallans, which is derived from the Central Scots language, known in Scotland as 'Inglis'. This Lallans language is still spoken in the north-east of Ulster and in Donegal, where contact with Scotland through settlement and commerce has been close. The Scottish speech is in some ways an older form of the English language grouping than standard English and R. de Bruce Trotter in his *Galloway Gossip* has listed the chief points of difference between the two grammars. [65] Church and state have been just as antagonistic to Lallans as they have been to Gaelic itself, leading to as great a contraction of the Scots-speaking districts as the Gaelic-speaking districts of Ulster.

An Incomplete Transformation   Yet Ulster as a whole was not anglicised as quickly as Leinster. According to the 1851 census, of the nine counties in Ireland which contained the least number of Gaelic speakers only one (County Down) was in Ulster — the other eight were in Leinster. Not only were there, at that time, twice as many Gaelic speakers in Ulster than in Leinster but each of the counties Antrim, Armagh, Londonderry, Fermanagh, and Tyrone contained more than either Carlow, Kildare, Wexford or Longford. Breandan O Buachalla has stated that in the 17th and 18th centuries there was extensive intermingling and intermarriage between the new Scottish settlers and the 'native Irish' so that by the 19th century "there existed in Ulster several population groups, apart from many individuals scattered here and there, partly of Irish and partly of Scottish origin, who were Irish in language and who belonged to one or other of the Protestant churches." Estyn Evans agrees that "There was much more intermarriage, with or without the benefit of the clergy, than the conventional histories make allowance for. Many planters became Catholics and many natives became Protestants. It is an emotional oversimplification to see the plantation in terms of ruthless Protestants seizing the best stretches of land and chasing the Catholics into the bogs and hills." [11] A.T.Q. Stewart indeed believes that "a very substantial proportion of the original population was not disturbed at all." [66] Furthermore, while the new settlers sought agricultural land they could cultivate, the preferred environment for the old traditional way of life was hill and bog-land, providing as it did both rough grazing for livestock and turf for fuel.

The fact that many 'native Irish' became Protestants is well illustrated by the Hearth Money Rolls for the Presbyterian parishes of Stranorlar and Leck in Donegal for the year 1665, as well as by the presence of such old Cruthinic families as Rooney, Lowry, Macartan and Maguinness in the records of the Episcopalian Diocese of Dromore in South and West Down. Representatives of well-known Gaelic families also abound. Murphys, Maguires, Kellys, Lennons, Reillys, Doghertys and many others are quite numerous. In this Diocese of Dromore and the immediately surrounding districts the Church of Ireland bears a larger proportion numerically to the total population than perhaps in any other part of Ireland of the same area. In North Down, where

17th century settlement from Scotland was most successful, Brendan Adams has stated that "a large part of the native population became absorbed into the Protestant Church." Thus in a book listing subscribers to church funds in the Presbyterian church in Saintfield, County Down, at least 20% of the names were native, pre-17th century names like Dugan, Donnan, Hanvey and Kelly. [67]

Ussher's *Discourse of the Religion anciently professed by the Irish* (London 1631) also shows that many Protestants in the 17th century felt that several important points of doctrine and discipline in the early Irish Church were closer to their own religious views than those of contemporary Roman Catholicism. These sentiments continued to be expressed by prominent Protestants down to modern times, notably by the Presbyterian historian James Seaton Reid in his *History of the Presbyterian Church in Ireland* (1833) and by the Gaelic scholar Nigel Mac Neill in his *Literature of the Highlanders* (1892). A great lover of the Bangor Antiphonary Mac Neill described the early Irish Church as "the primitive Free Church". For him there was no doubt that "The Gaels of Ireland and Scotland were the same people, having the same language and music; and all the elements of civilisation about them were the common property of both. At the same time there are evidences that the Gaels of the North of Ireland stood in closer relationship to those of Scotland than those in the South of Ireland. And this holds true even to this very day."

Uprising   However, although the plantation never proved to be the radical transformation the Crown might have originally intended, those Irish who were dispossessed had sufficient cause to harbour a deep-seated resentment. In 1641, with civil unrest in England between Parliamentarians and Royalists, an opportunity was offered to the Catholic Irish to redress the balance, and open rebellion was declared.

The plans for this rebellion were worked out by a member of one of the last Cruthinic families in Southern Ireland, the final remnants of the Loigse, who had held the territory named from them, Laois. The Loigse had been ruled by the Moores from the earliest documentary period until they lost their lands to English planters in the 16th century. It was primarily against the more recent, and therefore Protestant English settlers and the Dublin government that Rory O'More directed the first assault in October 1641. Prominent among his fellow conspirators were northern malcontents led by Sir Phelim O'Neill and with him was Sir Con Magennis of Iveagh. Within a few weeks the Anglo-Normans and other Hiberno-English of the Pale joined the insurrection on the side of the rebels.

It was the declared policy of the rebels at the beginning of the uprising that the Scottish Presbyterians should be left alone because of their 'Gaelic' origins. Thus Colonel Audeley Mervyn, in a report presented to the House of Commons in June, 1642, states that: "In the infancy of the Rebellion the rebels made open proclamations, upon pain of death, that no Scotchman should be stirred in body, goods or lands, and that they should to this purpose write over the lyntels of their doors that they were Scotchmen, and so destruction might pass over their families." Furthermore he related that he had read a letter, "sent by two of the rebels, titulary colonels, Colonel Nugent and Colonel O'Gallagher... which was directed to, 'Our honourable friends, the gentlemen of the never conquered Scotch nation'." However, the conflict quickly became a sectarian one, and the distinction between the Scottish and English Protestant settlers was not maintained. The English settlers suffered most, nevertheless, and many thousands lost their lives both in the fighting and in the privation which followed.

Catholic Army of Ulster   Not for the first time in Irish history a feeling of 'difference' was to be displayed between North and South, only this time, ironically, it was to be exhibited by Ulster's proud Gaelic chieftains. When Owen Roe O'Neill returned from exile to play a leading part in the Rebellion he encountered constant suspicion and intrigue from other Irish leaders, and formed his own 'Catholic Army of Ulster'. As Jerrold Casway writes in her biography of the Irish leader, "Rather than accept assistance from Owen O'Neill and the Ulster Irish, many Anglo-Irishmen preferred the Leinster forces... Owen and his northern army, they asserted, should remain in the north where they belonged." Rinuccini, the Papal Nuncio sent from Rome to assist the rebels, ascribed this animosity to "no other ends than the bad feeling which is cherished towards the men of Ulster." Indeed, when Rinuccini argued with a Munsterman who was 'a very good Catholic' that, rather than have heretics in Munster it was preferable to have Catholic soldiers from Ulster, he was told that this was not necessarily the case. [69]

Furthermore, Owen O'Neill "knew that the northern army was the only reliable and viable force of the native Irish, and without it he and his followers would be no better than seeds in the wind." [68] It was the Catholic Army of Ulster which fought the greatest battle of the war at Benburb. Before the battle Owen exhorted his men with a "Caesar-like oration", in which he told them: "You are the flower of Ulster, descended from as ancient and honourable a stock of people as any in Europe." Even Owen Roe himself could not have known just how true that statement was.

The rebels, despite forming themselves into a Catholic Confederacy, were disunited in their tactics and objectives, and loyalties on all sides were further complicated by the outbreak of Civil War in England between King and Parliament. And if this wasn't enough, by beheading the King in 1649, the Puritan government in England outraged and alienated their former Presbyterian allies in Scotland. These Presbyterians had entered into a 'Solemn League and Covenant' to protect their religion not so much against Catholicism but against the impositions demanded of them by the English High Church, and whatever political and religious grievances the 'Covenanters' may have harboured against Charles as King of England, he was also King of Scots, and more importantly a Stuart. The Stuart (Stewart) family had in the main line occupied the ancient throne of the Scots for upwards of three hundred years. This famous but ill-fated house sprang from a Brêton (Old British) nobleman named Alan son of Flaald who was contemporary with William the Conqueror.

In August 1649, with Irish resistance already on the wane, Oliver Cromwell landed in Dublin to take charge of the Parliamentary forces there, now reinforced by 2,000 of his Ironside veterans. Cromwell's intention was to restore this "Bleeding Nation of Ireland to its former happiness and tranquillity." However, little of this 'happiness and tranquillity' was to be engendered by his methods: his campaign was exactly what he intended it to be — quick and cruel, but effective.

Cromwell in Cromwell's campaign against the Royalist forces began with
Ireland the storming of Drogheda on 11 September 1649. The resultant massacre was directed primarily against the English Royalist garrison and the clergy. In October the Ironsides, now the finest army in Europe, took Wexford and, on finding evidence of atrocities committed against the town's Protestant inhabitants, gave no quarter to the Irish garrison. By the end of November the great Ulster leader, Owen Roe O'Neill, had died and the only Ulster strongholds left in Royalist hands were Charlemont and Enniskillen, while the Protestant Royalist garrisons of Cork, Youghal and Kinsale had joined Cromwell of their own volition. When Cromwell, the Lord Lieutenant and General for the Parliament of England, left Ireland on 26 May 1650 he was confident that his deputies would soon be able to finish the war, and that the Gaelic aristocracy was doomed, its caste system of social order destroyed for all time. Now Cromwell and his New Model Army could turn their attention to subduing his new adversaries, the Presbyterian Covenanters of Scotland.

Cromwell's designs for the conquered Ireland were embodied in an Act of Settlement passed by the 'Long Parliament' in England in August 1652. This provided for an extensive forfeiture of land in Ulster, Leinster and Munster, ten counties of which were set aside to remunerate the Parliamentary soldiers and those who had contributed funds to the war effort. While the leaders of the rebellion had forfeited all rights to their land and property, many others who had not "manifested their constant good affection to the Commonwealth of England" were to suffer partial forfeiture, losing one fifth, one third or two thirds of their estates, according to the degree of their "delinquency". A scheme was made whereby they would be obliged to accept lands in Connaught and Clare equal in value to the land which remained to them. The Irish prisoners-of-war were allowed to enlist in the service of European nations and about 40,000 did so, chiefly going to Spain. Some two hundred persons were executed for their parts in the massacre of 1641, among them Sir Phelim O'Neill. Catholic priests were transported to the West Indies. The Episcopalians also suffered, as did the Presbyterians of Antrim and Down, for it was decided that they should be transported south, away from the Scottish mainland and continued support from Ayrshire (Carrick) and Galloway. Cromwell indeed drove all the Anglican bishops out of Ireland and every Presbyterian minister with the exception of five.

Although it was first announced that all "transplantable" persons should remove themselves by 1 May 1654 and that they should be liable to death if they didn't, permission to delay for individuals was freely given. In April 1653, Cromwell dissolved the Rump Parliament and ruled as Lord Protector, and a change of policy towards the leading Ulster Scots meant that their transportation south was not carried into effect. Neither was the subsequent settlement of Ireland by Cromwellian soldiers a success, for not only did they need the Irish tenants but, despite strict attempts to prevent them, they intermarried with the Catholic Irish and within a generation many of them would become Catholics and fight for the Jacobite cause.

In 1645 Cromwell dispatched his son, Henry, to be ruler of Ireland and under his firm but mild government an increase in liberty was granted to Catholic, Presbyterian and Episcopalian alike, and Ireland began to prosper again. During the remaining years of the Protectorate the ministers of the devout Covenanting sect gained a tremendous hold over the people of Galloway and Ayrshire. This was to have a profound influence on following events. Ministers were allowed to return to Ulster. An Irish State paper of 1660 states that "there are 40,000 Irish and 80,000 Scots in Ulster ready to bear arms, and not above 5,000 English in the whole province besides the army."

The Subjugation of Galloway Following the death of Cromwell there was a year of turmoil, brought to a close by the restoration of Charles II in 1660. Charles's first act was to restore the Episcopalian Church in the Three Kingdoms, and in 1661 an Act of Conformity was passed which required every minister who officiated in a Parish church to confirm to the Episcopalian Church and the Prayer Book. 'Nonconformist' minsters were ejected from their churches, and the Parliament of 1662 confirmed the return of prelacy.

Throughout most of Scotland the ministers submitted, but not so in Galloway. There the people resisted and government troops were sent to occupy and terrorise the whole area. Courts of High Commission were reintroduced and hundreds of Covenanters were fined, imprisoned, tortured or deported to the Colonies. Eventually this could no longer be borne, and on 13 November 1666 the 'Pentland Rising' was initiated at Dalry. On 21 November a Covenanter force of about 1,000 men assembled at the Brig O'Doon near Ayr and marched on Edinburgh. On 28 November at Rullian Green, at the foot of the Pentland hills, they were routed, and many fled to Ulster and Holland. Following the Rising, the persecution of Galloway was increased under Sir William Bannatyne whose followers' murders, rapes and robberies were so numerous that the Government itself became sickened. In 1669 the Act of Indulgence was proffered to the Gallowegians, but it was not enough for them and only four ministers in the whole of Galloway subscribed to it.

In Ulster, on the other hand, the Presbyterians had learnt to live with the prelacy as they had done before and because of this Charles II was so well disposed towards them that he granted to the Ulster ministers a Regium Donum or Royal Bounty. So, for the twelve years following 1670, there was nothing that could be remotely described as persecution in Ulster. It was this difference between the two regions which resulted in an influx from Galloway of many of her impoverished citizens.

On 13 August 1670 the Scottish Government passed the notorious 'Black Act' which made field preaching an offence punishable by death. To this barbarous legislation the increasingly impoverished Hill Folk of Galloway uttered a defiance whose fire the Government attempted to extinguish in blood. In 1678 the arrival of the Highland Host under James Graham of Claverhouse marked the beginning of a grim final decade of persecution in Galloway. These Highlanders were "authorised to take free quarter, to seize all horses for carrying their sick men, ammunition and other provisions and are indemnified against all pursuits, civil and criminal. for anything they do whether killing, wounding, apprehending, or imprisoning such as shall make opposition to authority."

When the Highlanders returned to their homes at seedtime, as was the custom of such Gaelic raiding parties, their place was taken by English dragoons under their own officers, who gave orders to shoot on sight. On Sunday 1 June 1679 Claverhouse and his troops attacked a field meeting or conventicle at Drumclog, but was defeated by the Covenanters. On 22 June, however, a badly-led army of Covenanters were defeated at Bothwell Bridge. Following this a merciless persecution of Galloway was initiated. A Test Act was passed in August 1681 which obliged them to accept the complete authority of the King in all matters civil and ecclesiastical and to renounce Presbyterianism. Courts were set up to enforce this, and the innocent, suspected and guilty alike were subjected to extreme torture and then either imprisoned on the Bass Rock, or in Blackness Castle. Many others were transported to the colonies to be sold as slaves. Of these events Claverhouse wrote: "In the meantyme we quartered on the rebelles, and endevoured to destroy them by eating up their provisions, but they quickly preceived the dessein, and soued their corns on untilled ground. After which we fell in search of the rebelles, played them hotly with pairtys, so that there were severall taken, many fleid the country and all were dung from their hants; and rifled so their houses, ruined their goods, and impoverished their servants, that their wyfes and childring were broght to sterving; which forced them to have recourd to the safe conduct, and mid them glaid to renounce their principles."

In October 1684 James Renwick assumed the leadership of the Covenanters and published his 'Apologetical Declaration' against the king and his ministers. The Privy Council responded with an Act which stated: "The Lords of his majesty's Privy Council do hereby ordain any person who owns, or will not disown, the late treasonable document (the Apologetical Declaration), whether they have arms or not, to be immediately put to death." This opened the way for summary execution without trial and the following period, covering the autumn of 1684 and the whole of 1685, became known as the 'Killing Times'.

The growing prosperity and relative tolerance of Ulster during this period attracted not only many of the impoverished Galloway people, but also Puritans, Quakers and other Dissenters, mainly from the northern counties of England and especially from Yorkshire and Durham. These settlers were to leave their own impression on the language and personality of Ulster.

2 — The 'Glorious Revolution'

On 6 February 1685, Charles II of England died. When his brother James II ascended the throne the inhabitants of the growing town of Belfast (population around 2,000) sent a congratulatory address to the new King. But while "government in the last years of Charles II had been based upon a close understanding between the Court on the one hand and the High Church and Tory Party on the other," [70] James was an avowed Roman Catholic who was determined to adopt rapid methods of Romanizing the country.

The fears of the Protestant population in Ireland were first engendered by the recall of Ormonde, the Lord Lieutenant, whose Protestant sympathies were not in accord with James's design for the island. According to Lord Macauley, James also "obtained from the obsequious estates of Scotland, as the surest pledge of their loyalty, the most sanguinary law that has ever in our island been enacted against Protestant Nonconformists." [71] With this law and the dragoons of Claverhouse he wasted and oppressed Galloway still more, the atrocities culminating with the foul murder of the Wigton Martyrs, Margaret Maclachan and Margaret Wilson in May.

However, in England itself, before James could proceed with implementing any of his designs, a rebellion was raised by the Duke of Monmouth, natural son of Charles II, and a claimant to the throne. Among the radical exiles in Holland who financed his expedition was the great philosopher, John Locke. However, this ill-fated rebellion was crushed at the Battle of Sedgemoor on 15 July 1685. As G. M. Trevelyan wrote: "The revenge taken upon the rebels, first by Kirke and his barbarized soldiers from Tangier, and then by Judge Jeffreys in his insane lust for cruelty, was stimulated by orders from the King. It was the first thing in the new reign that alarmed and disgusted the Tories. In the general horror felt at the long rows of tarred and gibbeted Dissenters along the roadsides of Wessex, came the first recoil from the mutual rage of parties that had so long devastated English political and religious life, the first instinctive movement towards a new era of national unity and toleration." [70]

Although thus far triumphant, James's Catholic Design was ironically thwarted by anti-Protestant legislation enforced by his cousin, Louis XIV of France. The Revocation of the Edict of Nantes suppressed all the privileges granted by

Henry IV and Louis XII to the Huguenots, inhibited the exercise of the Protestant religion, enjoined the banishment of all its ministers with 15 days, held out rewards for converts, and prohibited keeping schools, or bringing up children, in any but the Catholic religion. Dragoons were sent into Languedoc, Dauphine and Provence to enforce the decree, and it has been estimated that some half-million Huguenots left France as a result. They migrated mostly to the British Isles, Holland and Germany, and brought with them their arts, industry and resentment. Their most persistent memories were the wholesale massacre of Huguenots on St Bartholomew's Day, 24 August 1572, by order of the Queen Mother, Catherine de'Medici, and the Siege of La Rochelle, 1628, where out of a population of 25,000 at least 10,000 died rather than surrender to the Catholic army under Cardinal Richelieu. This flood of persecuted Protestants into England made James's Romanizing intentions well-nigh impossible to implement.

But while in England James had to tread warily, in Ireland he felt he could progress as planned. In 1686 he appointed Richard Talbot, an ardent Roman Catholic, Earl of Tyrconnell and General of the Forces in the island. Tyrconnell proceeded to dismiss all 'Englishmen' from the army, disband the Protestant regiments and replace them with Roman Catholics. In January 1687 Tyrconnell became Lord Lieutenant of Ireland.

It was well known that Tryconnell's real intention was to drive all the recent settlers out of Ireland, to destroy the Protestant faith in general, and to restore the Irish aristocracy. (In May 1689 what is generally known as the 'Patriot Parliament', composed mainly of the 'Old English', or Anglo-Irish Catholics, would, against the opposition of James himself who looked upon his Protestant Irish subjects more pragmatically, repeal the Act of Settlement and pass an act of Attainder against some 2,400 Protestant landowners.)

While many of the Protestants prepared for the inevitable defiance others emigrated to England, where they further enhanced the fears of its Protestant majority as to James's intentions. However, the fears in England were not primarily religious. The Protestants feared the political implications of English Catholicism more than its theology; they feared the absolute nature of its claim to represent the ultimate in social order, more than its specific ceremonies; but most of all they began to fear for their country's parliamentary system of government.

As loyalty to James ebbed in England, so the civil power of Catholics increased in Ireland. By the autumn of 1688 all the judges in Ireland were Catholics as were almost all the highest officers of the State. On 5 November William Henry, Prince of Orange and Nassau, at the invitation of James's enemies, landed at Torbay in England with an army, and by the end of the year the King had abdicated and fled to France. Ironically, this development was welcomed by Pope Innocent XI, a man of moderation who disapproved of the policy being pursued by James, and who helped finance William's army. As G.M. Trevelyan pointed out: "Innocent had quarrels of his own with Louis

XIV and the French Jesuits; he dreaded the French power in Italy and in Europe, and therefore watched with sympathy the sailing and the success of William's Protestant crusade, because it would release England from the French vassalage. [William] was, himself, the head of a league against Louis that sought to unite Austria, Spain, and the Roman Pontiff with Holland and Protestant Germany. What the Pope and the moderate English Catholics hoped to obtain in England was not political supremacy but religious toleration."[70]

There was not, however, a similar constitutional crisis in Ireland where Tyrconnell still held the country firmly for King James. Even in Ulster the Presbyterians "did not at once appear against the king's government". According to J.M. Barkley, "What settled the issue was Tyrconnell's 'sparing neither age nor sex, putting all to the sword without mercy' (to use the words of a survivor) following the Break of Dromore." [72]

The Siege of Derry Meanwhile the regiment of Lord Mountjoy, which was one of the few essentially Protestant ones left, was ordered to leave Londonderry, which was to be garrisoned by the Catholic MacDonnells under Lord Antrim. The citizens, fearing a repetition of the events of 1641, wanted to refuse the troops entry. However, as Robert Kee points out: "Other voices, shocked, declared that it would be unthinkable to try and keep royal troops out of a royal garrison. The Protestant Bishop of Londonderry and other Protestant establishment figures were among the latter, although the Presbyterians with their naturally independent attitude to authority were less troubled by such scruples. The official decision, however, had been taken to admit the troops in the normal way, when suddenly thirteen apprentice boys of the city took matters into their own hands, seized the keys of the gates of Londonderry and on 7th December 1688 slammed them firmly in the face of lord Antrim's Redshanks — King James's troops." [59]

Enniskillen followed suit, and throughout Ulster, defence associations were set up and councils of war elected. On 13 February 1689 William and Mary (James II's Protestant daughter) were proclaimed King and Queen of England. The two were cousins. William's mother, Mary Stuart, was the eldest daughter of Charles I. William was thus also of Old British Royal lineage. On 12 March James II landed at Kinsale from France and marched north to destroy the latest affront to his authority. On 18 April he commenced the Siege of Londonderry, which lasted a total of 105 days, the longest in British history. During that time one third of the city's 30,000 inhabitants died of injuries, famine and disease. At last, on 28 July, Derry was relieved by the British ship *Mountjoy* and two other vessels.

Two aspects of the siege were to lodge deep within the Protestant subconscious: firstly, a 'No Surrender!' determination to stand firm against any perceived threats to their heritage; secondly, "an awareness that however much the northern Protestant may need British help he is also on his own" [59], a

70

feeling no doubt given weight by the fact that the British ships which finally lifted the siege had been nearby right from the beginning, but hadn't been able to summon up the courage to act.

Finally, on 14 June, 1690, King William himself landed at Carrickfergus and bonfires were lit on all the hills of Antrim and Down. At Loughbrickland in County Down William reviewed an army composed of Protestants from all over Europe — Dutch, Danes, French, Germans, English, Scots, Irish, Swiss, Italians, Norwegians and Poles. His army also included an elite unit, the Dutch Blue Guards, who were Catholics. The European dimension was to be completed by James's Jacobite force of Irish, French, English, Germans and Dutch.

The Boyne   On 1 July (celebrated as 12 July in modern calendars) the
and Aughrim   two armies met at the River Boyne, where William defeated
                           James's troops. When news reached Pope Alexander VIII, who was as delighted as his predecessor at what was in effect a French defeat, he ordered torchlight processions in Rome in celebration, and Te Deums were sung in the Catholic cathedrals of Austria and Spain.

Following the Battle of the Boyne the military position in Ireland remained fluid. The Boyne has been described as one of the decisive battles of the western world, for it signalled to Europe defeat for the French and the Jacobites — but it was not the final victory of the War. Neither was it a battle altogether characterised by the direction of the professional soldier but a magnificent drama portraying the personalities of the two kings each of whom caused problems for his own most able generals.

For if Sarsfield was betrayed by the cowardice of James, so Schomberg was dismayed by the almost foolhardy courage of William. The Prince of Orange's legendary bravery was linked to a strong, yet tolerant, religious conviction and a warm attachment to the Protestant faith, which sprang from earnest thought and attention. He possessed great military genius and soundness of judgement. At the Boyne his tactics were proved to have been correct. Yet, if the battle was won by William, the pursuit was not. The losses on both sides had been less than on any field of battle of equal importance and celebrity — fifteen hundred Jacobites and five hundred Williamites. Among the latter were Schomberg, the master soldier, and Walker of Derry, the heart and soul of his people. William's physical infirmities, his wound in the early part of the battle and the fatigue he had endured exhorting his men, had made him incapable of further progress. The King could not do everything, but what was not done by him was not done at all. And so the French and Jacobites escaped to fight another day.

From October 1690 until May 1691 no military operation on a large scale was attempted in the Kingdom of Ireland. During that winter and the following spring the island was divided almost equally between the contending parties. The whole of Ulster, the greater part of Leinster, and about one third of Munster were now controlled by the Williamites; the whole of Connaught, the greater part of Munster and two or three counties of Leinster were still held by the Jacobites.

Continuous guerrilla activity persisted, however, along the rough line of demarcation. In the spring of 1691, James's Lord Lieutenant, Tyrconnell, returned to Ireland, followed by the distinguished French general Saint Ruth, who was commissioned as Commander-in-Chief of the Jacobite army. Saint Ruth was a man of great courage and resolution but his name was synonymous with the merciless suppression and torture of the Protestants of France, including those of the district of Orange in the South, of which William was Prince.

The Marquess of Ruvigny, hereditary leader of the French Protestants, and elder brother of that brave Caillemot who had fallen at the Boyne, now joined the Dutch general Ginkell, who was strengthening the Williamite army at Mullingar. Ginkell first took Ballymore where he was joined by the Danish auxiliaries under the command of the Duke of Wurtemburg, and then the strategic town of Athlone.

Thus was the stage set for one of the fiercest battles of that age or any other. Determined to stake everything in a final showdown St Ruth pitched his camp about thirty miles from Athlone on the road to Galway. He waited for Ginkell on the slope of a hill almost surrounded by red bog, chosen with great judgement near the ruined castle of Aughrim.

Soon after 6 o'clock on the morning of 12 July, 1691, the Williamite army moved slowly towards the Jacobite positions. Delay was caused, however, by a thick fog which hung until noon and only later in the afternoon did the two armies confront each other. The Jacobite army of twenty-five thousand men had further protected themselves with a breastwork constructed without difficulty. The Williamites, numbering under twenty thousand, advanced over treacherous and uneven ground, sinking deep in mud at every step. The Jacobites defended the breastwork with great resolution for two hours so that, as evening was fast closing in, Ginkell began to consider a retreat. St Ruth was jubilant and pressed his advantage. However, Ruvigny and Mackay, with the Huguenot and British Cavalry, succeeded in bypassing the bog at a place where only two horsemen could ride abreast. There they laid hurdles on the soft ground to create a broader and safer path and, as reinforcements rapidly joined them, the flank of the Jacobite army was soon turned. St Ruth was rushing to the rescue when a cannonball took off his head. He was carried in secret from the field and, without direction, the Jacobites faltered. The Williamite infantry returned to their frontal attack with rugged determination and soon the breastwork was carried. The Jacobites retreated fighting bravely from enclosure to enclosure until finally they broke and fled.

This time there was no William to restrain the soldiers. Only four hundred prisoners were taken and not less than seven thousand Jacobites were killed, a greater number of men in proportion to those engaged than in any other battle of that time. Of the victors six hundred were killed, and about a thousand were wounded. If the night had not been moonless and visibility reduced by a misty rain, which allowed Sarsfield to cover the retreat, scarcely a Jacobite would have escaped alive.

Balldearg O'Donnell Waiting in the wings with his own army was a remarkable man named Balldearg O'Donnell. He had arrived from Spain shortly after the Battle of the Boyne claiming to be a lineal descendant of the ancient Gaelic kings of Tyrconnell in Ulster. He also claimed to be the O'Donnell 'with a red mark' (*ball dearg*) who, according to ancient prophecy, was destined to lead his followers to victory. Many ordinary Ulster Catholics had flocked to his standard, causing great hostility on the part of Tyrconnell who saw him as a threat to his own earldom.

Balldearg thus remained aloof from the battle. He proceeded to join the standard of William with 1200 men on 9 September, 1691, and marched to assist in the reduction of the Jacobite town of Sligo. This garrison surrendered on 16 September, 1691, on condition that they were conveyed to Limerick. Balldearg remained loyal to William and later entered his service in Flanders, with those of his men who elected to follow him.

With the surrender of Limerick on 3 October, 1691, the War finally ended and the 'Glorious Revolution' was complete. Most of the radical exiles in Holland, including Locke, returned to England as participants in, or in the wake of, the Revolution. Locke's Protestantism, which perceived humankind as constituting a spiritual community within which individuals were free, equal, endowed with reason, and capable of acting for the common good, sought to establish the basis on which society could progress to enlightenment. Furthermore, Locke's labour theory of property antedated by more than a century the economic debate which would come to dominate European political thinking. During William's reign the National Debt was commenced, the Bank of England established, the modern system of finance introduced, ministerial responsibility recognised, the standing army transferred to the control of parliament, the liberty of the press secured and the British constitution established on a firm basis. [73]

The Wild Geese James vindictively blamed his courageous soldiers for his defeat. "But it was their king that condemned the Irish to hopeless failure. He called them cowards, whereas the cowardice was really his own, and he deserted them in their utmost need. They repaid him with the opprobrious nickname of 'Sheemas-a-Cacagh', or Dirty James." [74] Many of the defeated Jacobite soldiers chose exile, and between 1691 and 1791 almost half a million such 'Wild Geese' left Ireland to form the famous Irish Brigades of armies throughout Europe, and of this number 50,000 fell in battle. James II's General, Patrick Sarsfield, Earl of Lucan, became a Marshal of France; Marshal Charles O'Brien, Viscount Clare and Earl of Thomond, fought for the French at Fontenoy; Marshal Count James Roland Nugent commanded in the Austrian army, and his son Laval became a Marshal in the service of King

Ferdinand V of Spain; Marshal Maxmilian von Browne rose in the service of Maria Theresa of Austria and Marshal Peter de Lacy became famous throughout Europe and parts of Asia as a commander in the Russian Army of Tsar Peter the Great.

Regional Identity   Once again, a sense of regional identity had been noted by those outsiders who had cause to be in Ireland during these times. A tract written on the Continent in the 1620s made it clear that Ireland was 'divided into two parts', North and South. As Raymond Gillespie and Harold O'Sullivan commented: "This division was reflected in differing attitudes and native Irish Ulstermen were by no means comfortable in seventeenth century Munster. George Storey, an officer in the Williamite army, noted in 1691 that after the war the Ulstermen who had fled to Kerry and Clare during the war began to return home 'which was a little odd to see' since it was a long journey, they had no assurance of regaining their farms in Ulster and there was a real risk of retaliation from the settlers. In contrast, land in Munster was cheap and available 'but', Storey noted, 'the reason for this is plain, for there is so great an antipathy between the Ulster Irish and those in other parts of the kingdom, as nothing can be more, and the feuds amongst them greater than between either and their injured protestant neighbours'." [75]

3 — The Scotch-Irish

The Protestants of Ulster had defended Derry and Enniskillen. They had saved Ireland for the British Crown. Yet all this passed for nothing. The English Church was Episcopalian and the 'Protestant Ascendancy' which now established itself in Ireland was thus actually an Episcopalian Anglo-Irish one, that is, the 'English in Ireland'. Having reduced the rebellious Catholics by the harsh Penal Laws under William, which were based on the French Catholic legislation against Protestants, the High Church Party had gained in strength, and by the reign of Queen Anne (1702-1714) were pressing for complete conformity.

In 1704 the Test Act was passed which required all office holders in Ireland to take the sacrament of the Anglican Church. Although ostensibly passed to further discourage Catholicism, the real object of the Act was to place the Presbyterians on the same plane of impotence. Presbyterian ministers had now no official standing and marriages performed by them were null and void. To the High Churchmen they were actually inferior to Catholic priests, who were considered lawfully ordained in the line of apostolic succession. Presbyterians and other Dissenters could not now serve in the army, the militia, the civil service, the municipal corporations, the teaching profession or the commission of the peace. At Belfast the entire Corporation was expelled, and Londonderry lost ten of its twelve aldermen (Schism Act).

74

Yet for all that, the Presbyterians had long made their adjustment to religious restrictions, and most bishops of the Church of Ireland were especially tolerant in an age of bigotry. Indeed, Archbishop William King was prominent in his expression of abhorrence to the Archbishop of Canterbury, not only of the risks of increasing alienation of the Presbyterians, but of English commercial avarice in restricting the Irish Woollen trade and the practice of rack-renting by landlords, whereby a farmer's land would be sold to the highest bidder when his lease ran out. The final straw came with the drought of the 'teen years of the 18th century. This ruined crops, including flax, so that farmers, weavers and townspeople suffered alike. In 1716 sheep were afflicted with the 'rot' and many died. Severe frosts ensued, prices soared and absentee English landlords steadily increased their rents. Thus began around 1717 the great migration from Ulster to America.

Into the New World An earlier emigrant to America was Francis Mackemie, born of Scottish parents near Ramelton, County Donegal. He settled in Eastern Virginia, and in 1706 was one of the most prominent members of the first Presbytery founded in America. Mackemie is justly considered to be the founding father of the Presbyterian Church in America, which was well organised to receive the new Ulster immigrants.

Soon Ulster people were settling in New York State, where they founded the Orange and Ulster counties. The first wave of migration to Pennsylvania (1717-1718) was enough to arouse the English conscience and in 1719 an Act of Parliament was passed to permit Dissenters to celebrate their own form of worship. But rack-renting continued and from 1725 to 1729 there was such an exodus of Ulster Presbyterians to the south-eastern tier of counties in Pennsylvania that their political influence was quickly becoming considerable. That influence was directed increasingly against England. A 'feed-back' into Ulster itself helped to make it a centre of radicalism, which was embodied in the establishment of one of the world's first daily newspapers, the *Belfast News Letter* in 1737. By 1738 Scotch-Irish settlers had pioneered their way from Pennsylvania into Virginia, of which two modern counties, Augusta and Rockbridge, claim to be the most Scotch-Irish in the present United States. By 1738 their Orange County, with its country seat in the Piedmont, embraced most of the Valley of Virginia, and also much of what is now West Virginia.

The winter of 1739-40 was known in Ulster as 'the time of the black frost', because of the darkness of the ice and the lack of sunshine. This severe weather caused famine all over the island, and a further wave of migration from Ulster (1740-1741). The new arrivals in America now generally went through Pennsylvania down into the Valley of Virginia. Here the McDowell family especially distinguished themselves, and thus did the Ulstermen become the men of Shenandoah. Others crossed the first range of the Alleghenies to settle in the valleys of (present) Highland and Bath counties.

The Scotch-Irish In *America's Historylands*, a celebration of the rich historical heritage of America, due acknowledgment is given to the pioneering efforts of these Ulster settlers:

> Immigrants first settled the over-mountain country: Germans, English, Highlanders, Irish, Welsh, Scotch-Irish. New England stock seasoned the mixture. Dominant were the Scotch-Irish, defiant and aggressive, who seldom neglected an opportunity to better themselves. They had undying confidence in their manhood, were as bold as the Romans, and as Indian fighters won even the Shawnee's admiration. They were Presbyterians, though in the wilderness many turned Baptist or Methodist. They believed in freedom and equality, resented class distinction and the leisurely life. They "preferred the useful to the beautiful and even required the beautiful to be useful." They contributed mightily to the democratization of the United States.

> Of Scotch-Irish stock was James Robertson, who founded a settlement (the site of present Elizabethton, Tennessee) on the banks of the Watauga River. For mutual protection against Indians and outlaws, the Wataugans in 1772 formed the first independent government established by white men west of the Appalachians. During the Revolution they placed themselves under the mantle of North Carolina, but had to beat off attack after attack by England's Indian allies. In 1779 Robertson recruited a party and led them down the frozen Cumberland River. On snow-covered bluffs they founded Nashboro (Nashville). After the war the Wataugans' Scotch-Irish blood boiled because North Carolina continued to ignore their needs, indeed referred to the settlers as "off-scourings of the earth". In 1784 the Wataugans resolved to break away, "forming ourselves into a separate government." [76]

The resulting State of Franklin kept its independence for four years before finally succumbing because of economic hardship. However, this one example of a Scotch-Irish settlement highlights the tenaciousness of purpose and the independence of attitude which these settlers brought to their new country of domicile.

The extent of Scotch-Irish settlement is well illustrated in this listing by W. F. Marshall: "Ulster's mark on America is also visible in its place names. There are eighteen towns in the United States named after Belfast. There are seven Derrys, nine Antrims and sixteen Tyrones. There is a Coleraine in Massachusetts. New Hampshire has Stewartstown. Washington, Ohio, and Iowa have each a Pomeroy. Hillsborough is in New Hampshire, Illinois, North Dakota, and Wisconsin. Maine has Newry. Ohio has Banbridge. In twelve States there are twelve Milfords." [77]

Destruction of the Indians While their ability to triumph over adversity speaks highly of the strength of character of the settlers, this uncompromising determination to establish themselves in their new land had a darker side to it — their ever-advancing settlements contributed greatly to the destruction of the Indian nation. The Indians were, as Fred A. Shannon explained, "a settled people, living in villages and practising an advanced stage of agricultural economy. They had many hundreds of cleared acres of land on which they grew corn, sometimes a hundred bushels to the acre, in addition to an equal amount of such vegetables as pumpkins, squashes, and beans. For lack of any indigenous animals that could be domesticated for draft purposes, hand implements were the only recourse for cultivation, but for several generations the white man (who looked upon them as savages because of their different complexion and habits) failed to excel these Indians in the quality of produce or the size of crops to the acre."

Throughout all the various Indian uprisings that punctuated the early history of America the central thread was to be the Indians' attempt to put a stop to the continuing white encroachments upon their lands. The Indians fought bravely, their most prominent victory being at the Battle of the Greasy Grass (Little Big Horn) River when Sitting Bull's braves wiped out General Custer's cavalry detachment in 1876, but more usually they suffered continuing defeats, including the infamous and needless massacre of nearly 250 Indian men, women and children at Wounded Knee Creek, in South Dakota on 29 December, 1890.

The Road to Revolution By the end of 1775 at least a quarter of a million Ulster men and women had left Ireland over a period of 58 years, and, according to some estimates, formed one sixth of the total population of the American Colonies. To America they brought a hatred of that aristocratic landlordism exemplified by the Marquis of Donegall, who had evicted many of the small farmers who couldn't pay the increased rents on his County Antrim estates. James Logan, the Provincial Secretary, had originally invited his fellow Ulstermen to Pennsylvania but soon complained that "a settlement of five families from the north of Ireland gives me more trouble than fifty of any other people." He found the Scotch-Irish "troublesome settlers to the government and hard neighbours to the Indians."

Indeed, the first armed clash to precede the Revolutionary War occurred in 1771 when Scotch-Irish settlers fought British forces on the Alamance River in North Carolina. On 20 May 1775 they were the most prominent signatories of the Mecklenburg Declaration of Independence drawn up in Charlotte, North Carolina. They subsequently supported the Declaration of Independence passed by the Continental Congress on 4 July 1776 and they composed the flower and backbone of Washington's army in the Revolutionary War which followed. Their cause was advocated by the *Belfast News Letter,* and the contemporary Harcourt wrote that "The Presbyterians in the north are in their hearts Americans." A German captain who fought alongside the British redcoats was quite explicit: "Call this war by whatever name you may, only call it not an American rebellion; it is nothing more or less than a Scotch-Irish Presbyterian rebellion." The Pennsylvania Line, the famous force of regular troops, was of primarily Ulster descent. George Washington said, "If defeated everywhere else I will make my last stand for liberty among the Scotch-Irish of my native Virginia." The birthplace of New York state was the Ulster County courthouse, burned in 1777 by the British, who were aided by the Iroquois Indians under their hero-chieftain, Brant.

Declaration of Independence The Official Declaration of Independence was written in the handwriting of Charles Thompson from Maghera, printed by John Dunlap from Strabane, given its first public reading by the son of an Ulsterman, Colonel John Nixon, and among the signatories were the following, all either born in Ulster, or born to Ulster parents — John Hancock, President of the Congress, Thomas McKean, Thomas Nelson, Robert Paine, Edward Rutledge, George Taylor, Matthew Thornton and William Whipple. The great Seal of the United States — an eagle holding arrows and a branch — was designed by Charles Thompson after a Congressional committee consisting of Franklin, Jefferson and Adams, broke up in disagreement. Edward Rutledge's brother John chaired a committee of five states which drew up the United States Constitution. According to Alexis de Tocqueville, the United States Constitution bore Rutledge's "personal stamp. One man made it; and it was Rutledge."

One direct influence on the radical thinking that was now being formulated in the 'New World' was the work of the great Ulster philosopher, Francis Hutcheson, son of an Armagh Presbyterian minister, and who was born probably at Drumalig, Saintfield, County Down in 1694. He studied for the church at Glasgow (1710-1716) but then started a private academy in Dublin where he was particularly associated with the advanced Presbyterian libertarians, Thomas Drennan, William Bruce and Samuel Haliday. In 1729 he was appointed professor of Moral Philosophy at Glasgow, where he died in 1746. His most important work is *A Sense of Moral Philosophy* (with a Life, 1755). Hutcheson was quite explicit about the right of resistance by the people in the event of a betrayal of trust by a government. He expounded the doctrine of religious toleration and he deeply admired the tradition of armed militias for the protection of civil liberties. The principles he espoused found their way via American revolutionary thinkers into the Declaration of Independence and are embodied in the American Constitution. Hutcheson's influence on Thomas Jefferson, John Adams and others is explored in M. White's *Philosophy of the American Revolution* and G. Wills' *Inventing America*. In fact, Wills concluded that Hutcheson's influence on Jefferson was stronger than that of John Locke. Hutcheson was a pioneer of the 'Common Sense' school of philosophy, influenced by Locke; his ethical system is a development of Shaftesbury's 'Moral Sense' ethics, in which moral distinctions are in a sense intuited, rather than arrived at by reasoning.

The most glaring omission from the Declaration of Independence was a strong disapproval of Black slavery. Had such a clause been included it would

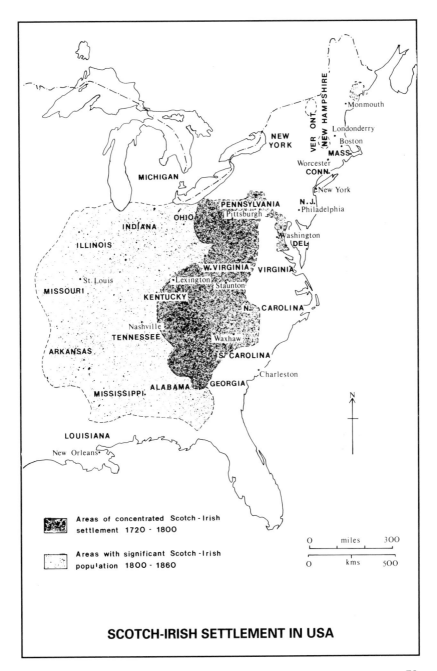

SCOTCH-IRISH SETTLEMENT IN USA

Areas of concentrated Scotch-Irish settlement 1720 - 1800

Areas with significant Scotch-Irish population 1800 - 1860

79

have made the way much easier toward final emancipation via legal methods. Matthew T Mellon, in his study of the racial attitudes of America's 'Founding Fathers', *Early American Views on Negro Slavery*, concluded that while the leading men at the time of the Revolution were all concerned with how to abolish the slave trade, economic pressures and moral indifference prevented them from energetically pursuing its abolition. "Problems grew out of the attitude of the early colonists and their European proprietors, who thought that the great natural resources of America were meant to be consumed and exploited as quickly and ruthlessly as possible. The English manufacturers realized that the slave trade, which began in the reign of Queen Elizabeth, was a great stimulant to American agriculture and would furnish raw material for their mills. On the other hand, the presence of the English markets and their ability to absorb all the raw materials that were produced, proved a stimulant to the plantation owners to increase their laborers. And while it is true, as Jefferson claimed, that the slave trade was imposed upon the colonists by powers outside of the colonies, it is also true that the colonists too quickly forgot their scruples against it. Any student of the period must admit that with the occasional outbursts of honest indignation against slavery and the slave trade there existed a great deal of moral indifference and unconcern which allowed this great social problem to develop."

"Remember the Alamo!"   The American expansion westward was pioneered by Ulster-Irish such as Davy Crockett and Jim Bowie. Sam Houston, also of Ulster descent, organised the rebellion of the Scotch-Irish settlers in Texas against the Mexicans and established the Republic of Texas. The famous Battle of the Alamo, fought in 1836, was viewed by the Texans as a heroic effort in their struggle for independence. Not unnaturally, President Antonio Lopez de Santa Anna of Mexico took a very different view and considered them traitors. The Texas Revolution of 1835-36 resulted from several grievances against Mexico, the most important being the subversion by Santa Anna of the 1824 constitution and his assumption of dictatorial powers. The Texans won the first battle at San Antonio, with the defeat of General Martin Perfecto de Cos on 10 December 1835, but Mexican forces numbering more than 6,000 appeared at San Antonio on 23 February 1836, and besieged the Alamo, a fortress near the town. The Alamo was defended by a force of 187 Texans, led by William Barrett Travis and including Davy Crockett and Jim Bowie. On 6 March the Mexicans made an overwhelming assault against the post and, on capturing it, killed all of the defenders. However, on 15 March Texas had declared her independence and Santa Anna's forces were defeated by the main Texas army under Sam Houston in April.

Ulster Music   Although the Scotch-Irish were merging quickly now into the American nation, the Ulster speech itself was to stay alive in the hill-country of Appalachia and beyond, where Scotch-Irish traditional music may still be heard. Among the earliest songs were ballads of King William of Orange, so those who sung them became known as Billy-boys of the hill country or 'hillbillies'. Rooted deep in the traditions of the British Isles peasantry, the fiddle had become an instrument of major importance in the development of Irish, Scottish and Welsh jigs, reels and hornpipes. As with folk custom in general, traditional music themes reinforced the ancient cultural divide between North and West Britain and Ireland, and South and East Britain. Transposed to America, the hoe-down fiddle reached the peak of its development in the Southern States. Musicologist W.H. Williams has written: "Ireland's initial impact upon American music came predominantly from Ulster... Whatever their influence in terms of cabin and barn styles, field layout, town planning, and so on, it seems likely that the greatest and most lasting contribution of the Scotch-Irish was music. And however one may define their particular religious and ethnic identity, musically they should be considered Ulstermen, for they brought with them the mixture of Scottish and Irish tunes which is still characteristic of large parts of Northern Ireland. When the great English folklorist Cecil Sharp went into the Appalachians to rediscover 'English' folk song, he was in fact often dealing with people of Ulster descent. Wherever they settled in large numbers and remained in relative isolation, balladry has been found 'live and in a healthy condition'." [79]

Civil War Leaders   The American Civil War of 1861-1865 was to produce a galaxy of military leaders on both sides who had Ulster and Irish lineage.

Ulysses Simpson Grant was Commander-in-Chief of the Union Army. He was the great-grandson of John Simpson who was born in 1738 at Dergina, near Dungannon, County Tyrone and left for Pennsylvania around 1760. Grant became President in 1868 and was said to preside over "more Ulstermen than Queen Victoria". He was well served by General Philip Henry Sheridan, the cavalry commander who outmanoeuvred the Confederate Commander-in-Chief Robert E. Lee and forced him to surrender at Appomatox on 9 April, 1865. Later he became Commander-in-Chief of the American Army. General Lee was once asked "what race makes the best soldiers?" To which the General answered: "The Scotch who came to this country by way of Ireland... Because they have all the dash of the Irish in taking a position, and all the stubbornness of the Scotch in holding it." The soldier of greatest reputation in the North for a considerable part of the war was General George B. McClelland, sometimes called "the pocket Napoleon". He was descended, on both his parent's side, from Ulster settlers of 1718.

On the Confederate side General Thomas 'Stonewall' Jackson, a simple God-fearing man, was outstanding and famed for his courage. His nom de guerre resulted from the heroic stand of his brigade at Bull Run on 21 July, 1861. He defeated the Union forces at Ball's Bluff and in the Virginian campaign of 1862 he routed them and followed up by invading Maryland. His great-grandfather came from Maghery on the shore of Lough Neagh. Only one man was victorious against Stonewall Jackson, and he was General James Shields, an Ulster Catholic, who was born in Altmore, County Tyrone, just thirty miles from the site of Stonewall Jackson's ancestral home.

The Civil War pitted family against family, kinsman against kinsman. W. F. Marshall has written: "On the Confederate side, North Carolina, home of the Ulster-Irish, led all the Southern States in enlisted men, and in killed and wounded. In the North, the pre-eminence goes to Pennsylvania, peopled in great measure by folk with the Ulster blood. The bloodiest single conflict of the war was fought between two regiments at Gettysburg, the 26th North Carolina Regiment and the 151st Pennsylvania Regiment.. Both regiments were practically wiped out. Well might Colonel Johnston say in 1889:'The greatest losses in the war occurred when the iron soldiers of North Carolina and Pennsylvania, descendants of the same race and stock, met on the field of battle, and locked arms in the embrace of death.' " [77]

A Unique Heritage The following United States Presidents have been of direct Ulster descent: Andrew Jackson (1829-37), James Knox Polk (1845-49), James Buchanan (1857-61), Andrew Johnson (1865-69), Ulysses S. Grant (1869-77), Chester Alan Arthur (1881-85), Grover Cleveland (1885-89 and 1893-97), Benjamin Harrison (1889-93), William McKinley (1897-1901), and Woodrow Wilson (1913-21).

Many other famous Americans have some Ulster ancestry, from writers such as Stephen Foster, Edgar Allan Poe and Mark Twain, to astronauts Neil Armstrong and James B. Irwin. John Hughes the first Catholic Archbishop of New York was born at Auger in County Tyrone, and emigrated to America in 1817, during a second great exodus from Ireland which occurred a century after the immigrations from Ulster, this second wave being mainly composed of Irish Catholics fleeing from a land devastated by the Great Famine. Hughes' successor and first American Cardinal, John McCloskey, was born in Dungiven in County Londonderry. There are many modern Americans who still take pride in their descent from Ulster-Irish families, though they often know little of Ulster itself. Not many of them are now Presbyterians, for most became Methodists and Baptists according to conscience. This was due to old-time preachers whose traditions also lived on in America's Black community to be personified by Martin Luther King. Yet, until recently, very little about the Ulster contribution to America was taught in our schools and universities. As Harold R. Alexander has written: "The migration of the Ulster people was a diaspora similar to that of the Jews. North America provided ample scope for the national character and soaring vision of men of Ulster origin... It is sad that almost nothing of this is known in Ulster today. English ascendancy and Irish chauvinism have combined to suppress knowledge of Ulster and Ulster-American history, to deny the very concept of the Ulster nation at home or overseas, and to deprive Ulstermen of legitimate pride in their heritage and national identity." [80]

James G. Leyburn's estimation of Scotch-Irish influence on the formation of the early United States includes the following assessment: "Weber's idea of the Protestant ethic and Tawney's of the connection between Protestantism and the rise of capitalism do not find their most convincing example in the Scotch-Irish; nevertheless, like other Calvinists, they believed in self-reliance, improving their own condition in life, thrift and hard work, the taking of calculated risks. They believed that God would prosper His elect if they, in turn, deserved this material reward by their conscientious effort. Farmers though they generally were, neither they nor their ancestors had been peasants in the sense of blind traditionalism of outlook. Their optimistic self-reliance, with a conviction that God helps those who help themselves, was to become the congenial American folk philosophy of the next century, not far removed from materialism and a faith in progress. The Scotch-Irish were no more the originators of these American convictions than they had been the originators of the idea of freedom and individualism. What is significant is that, holding the attitude they did, and being present in such large numbers throughout most of the United States, they afforded the middle ground that could become typical of the American as he was to become. The Scotch-Irish element could be the common demoninator into which Americanism might be resolved." [81]

4 — 'The Liberty Men'

The Volunteer Movement   The American Revolution was to have a profound effect on the further history of Ireland in general, and of Ulster in particular. When France and Spain joined the Americans in 1778, an invasion of Ireland was feared and an armed Militia was formed. These volunteers were predominantly Protestants, and they quickly became a political force in the fight for Irish Parliamentary independence. In Dublin, Jonathan Swift, the Protestant Dean of St Patrick's Cathedral, urged people to burn everything English except their coal! But it was in Belfast that those heights of radical political philosophy were reached which gave the town the name of 'Athens of the North'.

In February 1782 delegates from a number of Ulster Volunteer companies held a convention at Dungannon in County Tyrone and adopted resolutions favouring legislative and judicial independence and the relaxation of penal laws. In June of that year the Irish Parliament began to formally initiate its own legislation for the first time in over two hundred years. As Peter Smyth wrote: "It was appropriate that Ulster should have provided the final impetus towards achieving legislative independence. Ulster had almost as many Volunteers as the other three provinces combined, and a much higher proportion of its population was politically active. This population was well-leavened with the yeast of the Presbyterian tradition of independence of thought... Grattan and other politicians, declaring that 'Liberty is a native of the North', echoed the popular toast, 'May the Northern lights ever illuminate the Irish nation'. Such sentiments helped to foster Ulster's high opinion of itself as the arbiter of national aspirations." [82]

In 1784 the inhabitants of the town pressed for parliamentary reform and the emancipation of Roman Catholics. In 1789 they welcomed the French Revolution, while in 1791 they celebrated the second anniversary of the storming of the Bastille. However, when the new Parliament became hidebound through lack of proper reforms, the Volunteer movement went into a gradual decline.

The United Irishmen On 1 April 1791 a group of progressive thinkers met in Peggy Barclay's tavern in Belfast with the purpose of forming a society to promote the ideals that were inspiring so many of the Belfast radicals, men like Dr William Drennan, Robert and William Simms, Thomas McCabe, Henry Joy McCracken and Samuel Neilson. The natural extension of this meeting was the invitation to the young Dublin lawyer Theobald Wolfe Tone to come to Belfast on 14 October 1791, on which date was founded the Society of United Irishmen "to form a brotherhood of affection among Irishmen of every religious persuasion." Tone recorded in his Diary during his first visit to Ulster in July that Thomas Paine's *Rights of Man* had already become "the Koran of Blefescu", as he nicknamed Belfast in his private correspondence. In December the proclamation which led to the famous harpers' festival declared that "some inhabitants of Belfast, feeling themselves interested in everything which relates to the Honour, as well as the Prosperity of their country, propose to open a subscription which they intend to apply in attempting to revive and perpetuate the ancient music and poetry of Ireland."

The following year the United Irish Society established a radical newspaper, *The Northern Star*, in Belfast, edited by Samuel Neilson, the son of a Presbyterian minister.

In 1793 Britain declared war on France, and Pitt, the British Prime Minister, pressurised the Irish government to raise a largely Catholic militia to defend Ireland for the Crown. The Volunteers were at the same time disbanded by proclamation, and the proprietors of *The Northern Star* prosecuted. The Society of United Irishmen, or Liberty Men as they knew themselves, rapidly became a secret, oathbound movement dedicated to the overthrow of the state. In 1794 a Church of Ireland clergyman, the Rev William Jackson, landed in Ireland as an agent of the French government, and was captured the following year in possession of a paper which sketched a republican uprising. This paper described the Presbyterians of Ulster as "the most enlightened body of the nation". Jackson was charged with treason and executed in April 1795. Suspicion also fell on Wolfe Tone, who was thus forced to leave for America. Before he did do, he and the Northern leaders, Tom Neilson, Henry Joy McCracken and Thomas Russell, ascended the Cave Hill outside Belfast, where they swore to overthrow the power of England in Ireland for ever.

84

The Orange However, the American War of Independence had also closed
Society the door to further emigration from Ulster for the present, and
sectarian rivalry for land began to come into prominence again.
In September 1795, following a long period of disturbances, Catholic
'Defenders' attacked a notorious Protestant 'Peep o'Day Boys' tavern at the
Diamond in County Armagh, and were defeated in a pitched battle. Out of this
skirmish was born the Orange Society which was to develop later into the
Orange Order. In the autumn of 1796 a new force named the Yeomanry was
enlisted for the government in Ulster, and these were chiefly Orangemen.

Yet the majority of the Presbyterians of Ulster remained true to the ideals of
the United Irishmen, who had now received a new convert in the tragic young
Protestant aristocrat, Lord Edward Fitzgerald. In March 1797 the government
decided to disarm the North, and this was done with great cruelty by General
Lake. Belfast, in particular, suffered the scourge of the Catholic and Gaelic-
speaking Monaghan Militia. By May the whole island was put under martial
law, and many atrocities were committed both by British Army regiments such
as the 'Ancient Britons', a Welsh cavalry regiment, and the Orange Yeomen.
The latter were not a mass movement at this time but a small, mostly agrarian
society who represented the interests of the landed gentry, particularly in
Monaghan and Armagh. It is doubtful, however, if United Irish feeling would
have remained strong in Ulster if it had not been for the hanging of one of the
Presbyterian leaders, William Orr, in September 1797. 'Remember Orr' was a
slogan as long imprinted on the hearts of Antrim as was 'Betsy Gray' later on
the 'Hearts of Down'.

The Year of The year of 1798 was to be the First Year of Liberty for the
Liberty United Irishmen. They had now some half-million members of
whom about one half were armed, and of these 100,000 were
Ulstermen and two-thirds of these were Presbyterians. The Rebellion of '98,
however, was doomed from the outset. The Northerners realised that they
could accomplish little without foreign aid, and this was too slow in coming
from the French and their Dutch allies. The almost 'American' Presbyterians
were increasingly distrustful of France when she quarrelled with the United
States early that year. Furthermore, the arrest of most of the Leinster leaders of
the United Irishmen in March, 1798, followed two months later by their
successors, robbed the rebellion of truly United Irish leadership. In particular
the arrest of Lord Edward Fitzgerald and the Sheares brothers placed the
Leinster forces under Catholic, and often priestly, control.

Henry Joy The leadership of the Ulster rising was placed in the hands of
McCracken the young radical, Henry Joy McCracken, who was from a
well-known Belfast merchant family. Thomas Packenham
describes McCracken as "a remarkable man — in many ways the most attractive
of all the original United brotherhood in Ireland. He displayed none of the

defects of the others: the amiable fecklessness of Lord Edward, the impossible arrogance of Arthur O'Connor, or the stern self-righteousness of Thomas Addis Emmet. By birth a Presbyterian and by temperament a crusader, he had taken at once to the new philosophy of liberty and equality. He identified himself, as few of the movement's leaders did, with a demand for social justice. For him political and religious liberty, and national independence itself, were only means to that end. This, together with his personal magnetism, his diplomatic skill and his obvious enthusiasm, had suddenly thrust him into the front of the movement in the North." [83]

His progressive thinking had already led McCracken to confront the establishment in Belfast. In 1788 he and some friends voluntarily organised education classes for the working class of Belfast, who were being denied such education because of their poverty. Interference from the Town Sovereign, Rev William Bristow, compelled them to cease this experiment, but McCracken soon afterwards established a cheap lending library in opposition to the Belfast Reading Society, whose charges were so high that only the rich could afford to borrow books.

United Army of Ulster When hostilities finally broke out on 24 May, they quickly took on the character of a religious and bloody war in the south. In the North, McCracken managed to rally twenty-five Antrim regiments numbering some twelve thousand men, with as many again from Down, supported by contingents from Tyrone and Armagh. He addressed his men in confident tone: "Army of Ulster, tomorrow we march on Antrim; drive the garrison before you and haste to form a junction with your Commander-in-Chief."

McCracken's confidence was misplaced. The Ulster Presbyterians were dismayed by the lukewarm support from the Northern Catholics, and then horrified by the stories of atrocity and massacre of Protestants at Scullabogue on 5 June. Nevertheless, on 7 June, the United Army of Ulster took Larne and Antrim, but was soon defeated and Henry Joy captured. On 9 June the 'Hearts of Down' won the Saintfield skirmish and proceeded to Ballynahinch, where on 13 June they were decisively defeated and their leader Henry Munro captured and hanged.

On 17 June the noble Henry Joy was executed in Belfast. His devoted sister Mary Ann wrote lovingly of his last moments:

> I took his arm and we walked together to the place of execution, where I was told it was the General's orders that I should leave him, which I peremptorily refused. Harry begged I would go. Clasping my hands around him, (I did not weep till then) I said I could bear anything but leaving him. Three times he kissed me and entreated I would go; and, looking round to recognise some friend to put me in charge of he beckoned to a Mr Boyd, and said 'He will take charge of you.'... and fearing any

further refusal would disturb the last moments of my dearest brother, I suffered myself to be led away. [84]

As Packenham commented, McCracken was "a gentle, idealistic man, and determined that the rising in the North, at any rate, would not be disgraced by a counter-terror in the name of liberty. And to this principle he remained true in all the horrors of the succeeding week. In contrast to the wild scenes in the South, the northern United men acted with notable restraint [during] the short-lived Republic of Ulster." [83]

Thus did the rebellion in Ulster collapse.

Sectarian Tragedy In Wexford there had been more success, but its sectarian nature had little to do with United Irish ideals. The seal of ignominy was set on the Southern movement when 100 Protestant captives were slaughtered indiscriminately at Wexford on 20 June. Paradoxically it was among the loyalist ranks that sectarian animosities were overcome. The Catholics of the militia and yeomanry fought side by side with Orangemen and the force which had contained the rebellion in June was an overwhelmingly Catholic one. Urged on by their leaders, who were of the Protestant Ascendancy class, the Catholic Monaghan Militia were not content with defeating the Liberty men of Antrim and Down, but burned and pillaged everything in sight, including the entire town of Templepatrick. The *Belfast News Letter* of 15 June 1798 reported that they had retired laden with booty.

By the time the French arrived at Killala Bay, County Mayo, in August and at Lough Swilly in September, the rebellion was virtually over. Both these expeditions were defeated and Tone, who was with the latter one, was captured. Rather than be hanged the brave idealist committed an honourable suicide.

Rory Fitzpatrick gave this assessment of the Rising in the North: "The '98 Rebellion in Ulster was ill-conceived, badly organised and ultimately pointless, but it sprang from generous hearts and the rebels died with hardly a blemish on their name. The Presbyterian community gave some of their brightest and best in a cause that was only partly their own. The patriotism which inspired the Ulster rebels was a broad one, concerned with the rights of human beings and social justice rather than narrow tribal interests. It had nothing in common with the 'ourselves alone' approach of the later Catholic nationalism." [85]

The Union Ironically, the failure of the Rebellion led directly to an Act of Union being passed, and on 2 January 1801 Ireland became part of the United Kingdom. This new Union between Great Britain and Ireland was seen by several of the imprisoned United Irish leaders as actually an achievement of some of their aims and an admission by the Westminster Parliament that the Irish Parliament had been corrupt and unjust. In 1799 Samuel Neilson had written from Fort George prison in Scotland: "I see a Union is determined on between Great Britain and Ireland. I am glad of it. In a commercial point of view, it cannot be injurious; and I can see no injury the country will sustain from it politically." Another '98 leader saw in the Union "the downfall of one of the most corrupt assemblies I believe ever existed, and instead of an empty title, a source of industrious enterprise for the people."

As for the Ulster Protestants, disgusted, dismayed and finally fearful of the new sectarian aspect of 'Irish Freedom', many joined the Orange Order, which ironically opposed the Union Act, fearing Catholic emancipation. It is noteworthy that not a single Orange resolution in favour of the Union was passed in Ulster. In 1802 one of the '98 leaders, Thomas Addis Emmet, met the First Consul of the French Republic, Napoleon Bonaparte, who promised him aid. Article One of Emmet's revolutionary proclamation provided for the confiscation of all church property, an idea not entirely relished by the Irish Roman Catholic hierarchy. Emmet's brother Robert planned a new rebellion in 1803, but this was poorly organised and ended in debacle. Among those who turned out with the Dublin Lawyer's Yeomanry Corps to hunt down the rebels was a young man named Daniel O'Connell.

New Class Awareness   The United Irish movement had been an unusual alliance of classes. The Presbyterian leadership were predominantly middle class, while the rank and file membership in the South were from the Catholic peasantry. Although this joining together of forces must have delighted those who strove to unite 'Protestant, Catholic and Dissenter', the barely-developed political consciousness of the period no doubt prevented many of the participants from realising the inherent instability and contradictions within such an alliance, especially when we take into account that both groupings would have held widely differing perceptions of just what was meant by 'Liberty' and 'Equality' — to the Protestant middle class it would have meant 'political' liberty and 'commercial' equality, while for the Catholic peasantry, with their precarious subsistence lifestyle, it would have meant something much more fundamental.

Not that all the United Irish leaders were remote from the social realities of the period. One of them, Jemmy Hope, a hand-loom weaver from Templepatrick who taught himself to read and write, was well aware of the contradictions. He had sensed that in some quarters the movement for reform was "merely between commercial and aristocratical interests, to determine which should have the people as its prey... None of our leaders seemed to me perfectly acquainted with the main cause of social derangement, if I except Neilson, McCracken, Russell and Emmett. It was my settled opinion that the condition of the labouring class was the fundamental question at issue between the rulers and the people." [86]

Hope began his political career by joining the Roughfort Volunteers, and then in 1795 the Liberty Men. His great ideal was to help create a movement which would restore to the people their natural right — "the right of deriving a subsistence from the soil on which their labour was expended." With such views Hope had obviously gravitated towards McCracken. As Mary McNeill wrote: "It is not surprising that between Henry Joy McCracken and Jemmy Hope there arose a bond of deep attachment and confidence: here was the leader who cared nothing for privilege and possessions and everything for the advancement of the labouring man; here, on the other hand, was the labouring man possessed of an unusually alert and sensitive mind, able and willing to put theories into practice. There is little doubt that they learned much from each other." [84]

Between 1795 and 1798 Hope travelled widely throughout the island organising the working people. A member of the United Army of Ulster he played a leading part in the Battle of Antrim and distinguished himself under difficult circumstances. After the defeat of the Rising he pursued both his trade and his politics in Dublin, returning to Belfast in 1806. James Hope remained convinced of his ideals until he died at Brown Square, off the Shankill Road in Belfast, in 1847. His name is commemorated in Hope Street, Sandy Row, Belfast.

5 — Modern Ireland

During the Napoleonic Wars which followed Irishmen of all persuasions fought together in the British Army. New regiments, such as the Connaught Rangers, fought like heroes alongside the famous Inniskillings, and it was such men whom Arthur Wellesley, first Duke of Wellington, had in mind when he said: "It is mainly due to the Irish Catholics that we all owe our proud pre-eminence in the military career." Indeed, it has been estimated that at least half of the British Army at Waterloo in 1815 were Irishmen. Certainly, according to Wellington, himself the most British of Irishmen, "the 27th of Foot (Inniskillings) saved the centre of my line at Waterloo". Speaking in the House of Lords as Prime Minister of England in 1829 in support of the Catholic Emancipation Bill, he praised at length and with much eloquence the Irish soldiers who had served under his command in the Peninsular War and in Flanders. Another great Irish soldier of the period was Bernardo O'Higgins who liberated Chile and then served as its President from 1817 until 1823.

Daniel In 1823 Daniel O'Connell formed the Catholic Association, and
O'Connell within six years Catholic Emancipation was achieved. The
organisation of a national police administration in the 1830's took power away from the Orange Order. Following an attack on the Order by the great British radical John Hume in 1836 the Grand Lodge formally dissolved itself and its influence declined. In April 1840 O'Connell formed the National Repeal Association backed by the reactionary Archbishop of Tuam. Early support for this also came from the mainly Protestant 'Young Ireland' movement, whose ideals were those of '98. Disillusionment with conservative Catholicism

came for the Young Irelanders when McHale of Tuam and the bishops insisted that Roman Catholic students at the newly founded Queen's Colleges could not attend lectures on history, logic, anatomy, geology, metaphysics or moral philosophy "without exposing their faith and morals to imminent danger", unless the lecturers were Roman Catholics. Furthermore, O'Connell's call for a "Catholic parliament for a Catholic people" signalled the rebirth of Catholic nationalism, that independent form of Irish Nationalism, alien to the ideals of '98, which brought back bitter memories of Catholic sectarianism to Ulster's Protestants. For O'Connell, Protestants were "foreigners to us since they are of a different religion".

The Great Famine However, an event was now to occur which was to change the social, economic and ultimately the political history of Ireland.

The failure of the staple potato crop led to the Great Famine of 1845-49, probably the single most traumatic event in the island's history, striking right to the very heart of Irish life. Up to a million of the starving and disease-ridden population would perish. The total demoralisation engendered by the tragedy not only dealt a near-fatal blow to the lingering beliefs in the 'protective magic' of the ancient Elder Faiths — which were still patently strong — but lent new impetus to the upsurge of nationalist sentiment.

As if the loss of life caused by the Famine was not enough, Ireland was to lose a further million citizens during the massive emigration which followed. Many did not get beyond Glasgow and Liverpool. Other emigrants formed in the U.S.A. an unwanted nation within a nation, the Irish-Americans, whose influence on the further history of Ireland was profound.

Following the American Civil War (1861-65), the Irish-Americans formed a recruiting source for the violent anti-British Fenian movement. Founded in 1858 by James Stephens, who had fought in the Young Ireland rising of 1848, the Fenian Brotherhood saw themselves as the inheritors of the ideals of Tone and Davis. Believing that they could provoke an Anglo-American confrontation which would provide an opportune setting for revolt in Ireland, a party of Fenians made a raid on Canada in 1866. This was unsuccessful, as was an Irish uprising in 1867, and further invasion of Canadian territory in 1870 and 1871.

The bravery and tenacity to the ideals of '98 shown by the Young Irelanders and Fenians influenced a former Unionist, Isaac Butt, who had spoken against Daniel O'Connell in his youth, to form the Home Government Association. A member of Committee of the Grand Orange Lodge of Ireland, Butt's conservatism was supplemented by a great love of his country. One of the first Ulstermen to join the Home Government Association was John Madden, brother of a prominent Monaghan Orangeman. Madden felt alienated by Episcopalian disestablishment. The Home Government Association gradually grew in acceptability and size so that it became necessary to reconstitute the movement. The Home Rule League was therefore formed in 1873. As Christopher McGimpsey has explained, "This was the turning point and the evolution of Home Government Association to Home Rule League was also the movement away from aspects of Orange Home Rule and Protestant élite nationalism into a more O'Connellite, popular, democratic and Catholic movement." [87]   After the election of 1874, Butt led a revamped Home Rule Party in the Westminster parliament.

The Road to The 1870's and 1880's, however, became known as the age of
Home Rule Charles Stewart Parnell, who linked the cause of land reform with that of Home Rule, and moulded the Irish Parliamentary Party into a powerful force. To the Protestants of the North Parnell's association with the Fenian Brotherhood (Irish Republican Brotherhood) had sinister implications, and this led to a revival of the Orange Order, which became a truly popular movement, combining Episcopalians and Presbyterians, Conservatives and Liberals, landlords and tenants, employers and workers, in a fierce opposition to Home Rule.

Before 1885, there had still been a significant liberal element within the Ulster Protestant community, many of whom identified with an Irish heritage which belonged to *all* the people of Ireland. Indeed, the survival today of a large body of Gaelic literature written in Ulster between 1600 and the end of the 19th century is largely due to the interest taken in the material by prominent Ulster Protestants.

However, the resurgence of Catholicism following the Great Famine and the unfortunate abandonment of the old Belfast idea of a common Irish identity in favour of O'Connell's Catholic nation convinced many Protestants that Home Rule could only promote the power and the influence of the Catholic Church, and so 'Home Rule' became synonymous with 'Rome Rule'. Finally, the crisis brought about by the British Prime Minister Gladstone's declaration in favour of Home Rule instantly swept all sections of 'loyalists' into one camp. After 1886 the Orange Order expanded to become the mass movement of Unionism and the voice of organised Protestantism.

Commenting on the fears raised by the spectre of Home Rule, Rory Fitzpatrick has written:

"There was a widespread assumption that Home Rule would mean the greatest eviction that Ireland had ever seen — the turning-out of the Scots-Irish from their lands, their factories and their homes. Ulster was filled with rumours of Protestant property being raffled at Catholic churches in anticipation. 'Lots were drawn,' says Frankfort Moore, 'for certain houses, with the grounds, timber and livestock.' In Belfast, people living in the more prosperous part of the city 'were surprised to come suddenly upon strangers measuring their lawns and examining their fences'.   One householder politely asked an intruder what he was doing: 'The man replied with equal civility, that he had merely come to have a good look at the place, as he had been fortunate enough to win it in the raffle... by the Nationalist club.' No doubt the impracticalities of an immediate wholesale expropriation of Ulster-Scots property — a reversal of the Plantation settlement — was realised at the higher levels of nationalist leadership, but within the Catholic rank and file the expectation was there. Not since 1641 had so many spectres stalked the Ulster landscape. A British Prime Minister was preparing to sell the Ulster Protestants for a handful of parliamentary votes. They would be ruled by a Catholic administration in Dublin, with Catholic judges and a Catholic police; they would lose the industries which had made Belfast a great city (the chairman of the Belfast shipyard said he would move his firm to Scotland if Home Rule came about); and looming very close to them now was the menacing figure of the now infallible Pope whom they — and many Catholics — believed would be the real ruler of Ireland." [85]

The Rise of Gaelic Nationalism   In 1884 the Gaelic Athletic Association had been formed, which promoted hurling and Gaelic football and forbade the playing of "foreign games". In 1893 the Anglican Douglas Hyde co-founded the Gaelic League, which had as its aim the 'de-Anglicization' of Ireland. From this sprang Gaelic nationalism: "Ireland not free only, but Gaelic as well; not Gaelic only, but free as well." Strangely enough, through the Anglo-Irish poets Yeats and Lady Gregory, a pseudo-Celtic Twilight Culture was created, which not only bowdlerised, but Anglicised the old Gaelic literature out of all recognition. The political manifestation of the 'Gaelic Revival' was the foundation of 'Sinn Fein' (*Ourselves Alone*) in 1905. This movement soon attracted and was taken over by the veteran Fenians. At the same time there was a growth of Marxist philosophy, and an active socialist movement was led by James Connolly and James Larkin. Connolly, however, tried to use Gaelic nationalism to further his own ideals, thus compromising the Labour movement in both Ireland and Britain. The blending of Roman Catholic and 'Celtic' mysticism created in people as diverse as Patrick Pearse and James Connolly the myth of the blood sacrifice, which was to have lasting consequences.

Perceiving all these forces as threats the Northern Protestants formed an Ulster Unionist Council to resist Home Rule. Civil War now seemed inevitable. In 1912 almost half a million Ulster Protestants signed a 'Solemn League and Covenant' whereby they swore to use "all means which may be found necessary to defeat the present conspiracy to set up a Home Rule parliament in Ireland." 1913 saw the formation of the Ulster Volunteer Force under Sir Edward Carson and Sir James Craig, the Irish Citizen Army under James Connolly and the Irish Volunteers under Eoin MacNeill of the Gaelic League. Irishmen were girding themselves for the approaching conflict.

When the Ulster Volunteer Force was formed, Eoin MacNeill, President of the Irish Volunteers, tried to paint an optimistic picture of this marshalling of Northern Protestant forces: "A wonderful state of things has come to pass in Ulster... The Ulster Volunteer movement is essentially and obviously a home rule movement. [It is] the most decisive move towards Irish autonomy since O'Connell invented constitution agitation. It claims, no doubt, to hold Ireland 'for the Empire'; but what really matters is *by whom Ireland is to be held.*" [88] However, few could have been so easily beguiled, even MacNeill himself, by the seriousness of the situation now developing. And yet, ironically, the conflict that would soon fall upon them would be of European, not of Irish, making, for on 4 August 1914 Britain declared war on Germany.

The Great War   The First World War presented many dilemmas to the Irish. While most Protestants wanted to fight for Britain, some doubted if they should be directing their energies towards European battlefields when the situation in Ireland was still so uncertain. Many Catholics also wished to aid Britain, while others felt that England's difficulty was Ireland's opportunity. Yet, in the event, both parties to the Irish conflict declared their willingness to join with Britain, each hoping to be rewarded for their loyalty, even if their respective rewards couldn't have been any more dissimilar. From all parts of Ireland men came forward in their thousands to enlist. In some towns the Ulster Volunteers marched side by side with the Irish Volunteers to send off departing troops.

Carson won his argument to have the Ulster Volunteer Force kept together as a unit, and it was reorganised as the 36th (Ulster) Division. Irish Catholics, including many from Ulster, enlisted in the newly formed 10th and 16th (Irish) Divisions. Little could these eager recruits have realised that within four years 50,000 of them would have given their lives in the conflagration which was to follow.

The 10th (Irish) Division was the first to be well-blooded, fighting gallantly at Sedd-el-Bahr and Suvla Bay during the ill-fated landings in the Dardanelles. Of that particular episode Brigadier-General W.B. Marshall has written: "Though I am an Englishman, I must say the Irish soldiers have fought magnificently. They are the cream of the Army. Ireland may well be proud of her sons. Ireland has done her duty nobly. Irishmen are absolutely indispensable for our final triumph." Captain Thornhill, of the New Zealand Force, said: "Your Irish soldiers are the talk of the whole Army. Their landing at Suvla Bay was the greatest thing that you will ever read of in books. Those who witnessed the advance will never forget it."

The Battle of the Somme   In France the human tragedy of Verdun would soon dispel any doubts that may have remained by then that modern warfare, particularly as it was fought out in the mud-filled trenches, was anything other than a man-made obscenity. As the intense German pressure on the French army at Verdun took an ever-increasing toll not just in young French lives but on the very fighting spirit of a once proud army, a new offensive was launched to see if the deadlock could be broken. The place chosen for this offensive was the River Somme.

On the morning of 1 July 1916 a hundred thousand Allied soldiers left their trenches and began a lonely walk across the no-man's-land which separated them from the German positions. By the end of that day the British Army had suffered 60,000 casualties, 20,000 of them killed — the greatest loss ever suffered in a single day by the British Army or by any army in the First World War. The 36th (Ulster) Division was one of the few units to achieve its objectives that day, yet not only was their gallant success not followed up, but the price they paid was high – with casualties of over five thousand five hundred officers and men, the dead accounting for half of this number.

As Captain W.B. Spender wrote: "I am not an Ulsterman, but yesterday, the 1st July, as I followed their amazing attack, I felt that I would rather be an Ulsterman than anything else in the world. My pen cannot describe adequately the hundreds of heroic acts that I witnessed... The Ulster Volunteer Force, from which the Division was made, has won a name which equals any in history. Their devotion deserves the gratitude of the British Empire."

It was some days before the closely-knit communities in Ulster became aware of the extent of the sacrifice in young lives. As A.T.Q. Stewart wrote: "In the long streets of Belfast mothers looked out in dread for the red bicycles of the telegram boys. In house after house blinds were drawn down, until it seemed that every family in the city had been bereaved." [89]

A few months later it was the turn of other Irishmen to be flung into the battle, this time the men of the 16th (Irish) Division. This Division included five Ulster battalions and also the 6th Battalion The Connaught Rangers, which contained over 600 Ulstermen recruited mainly from the Falls Road district of West Belfast. The 16th Division is most prominently identified with the capture of the villages of Guillemont and Ginchy.

In his history of the Great War, Frank A. Mumby described the Irish effort: "Our greatest success [on the 3rd September 1916] was the capture of Guillemont by the Irish troops. They advanced on Guillemont with an impetuosity which carried all before it: charged through the German positions with the wild music of their pipes playing them on. Before the afternoon was out the 2000 Prussians who constituted the garrison — with imperative orders to hold the ground at all cost — were killed, wounded, or captured... The same Irish troops charged into Ginchy as they had charged into Guillemont, through the barrage of shells and the storm of machine-gun fire, clambering over shell-holes, fallen trees, and the great mounds of bricks and rubble which were all that remained of the village itself; cheering like mad, and driving the enemy before them in a fierce assault against which nothing could stand." [90]

Altogether the Battle of the Somme dragged on for four and a half months — a series of offences in a savage war of attrition which resulted in more than 400,000 British casualties for an advance of only six miles. Yet German casualties were probably as high as 700,000 and constituted a severe blow to the German Army. The irony was that soon after the battle ended, the Germans withdrew to the newly constructed Hindenburg Line, giving up ten times more ground than was won at such a cost in 1916. Furthermore, during the German offensive of March 1918, their Army swept over the old Somme battlefield in one day. It is scarcely surprising, therefore, that the Battle of the Somme came to exert such a strong hold on the popular imagination, albeit largely based on myths perpetuated by those who wished to apportion blame for the failure of the offensive, in particular the then Prime Minister David Lloyd George, who had political motives for attacking the generals' conduct of the war.

In Ulster, the Somme came to hold a special place in the national consciousness of ordinary people, comparable to that of Gallipoli to the Australians and New Zealanders, Vimy Ridge to the Canadians and Delville Wood to the citizens of South Africa.

Messines On 7 June 1917 the Battle of Messines took place, the first completely successful single operation on the British front, and as H.E.D. Harris has pointed out: "It is also memorable to Irishmen as largely an all-Irish achievement; two of the three divisions in the attacking line were Irish, the 36th on the right and the 16th in the centre of IX Corps, a unique line-up of Irish fighting men, and the largest in modern history. They showed to the world the sight of nearly 30,000 Irishmen shoulder to shoulder, men of all four provinces, and the only rivalry that existed between them was that of gallantry. In his book *As from Kemmel Hill*, Andrew Behrend wrote: 'I should like to put on record one further memory of the Battle of Messines. However little it interested me then, it fascinates me today, that during this battle and for weeks before, the 16th (Irish) and the 36th (Ulster) Divisions lived and fought side by side, got on with each other splendidly and at times even pulled each other's chestnuts out of the fire...'." [91]

A year later, both Divisions were to receive yet another battering. As Brigadier A.E.C. Bredin commented, the 16th and 36th Divisions "suffered the heaviest losses of any formation during the great German offensive of March, 1918." [92]

A genuine comradeship-in-arms had developed between many Irishmen because of their experiences during the war, but the political situation to which they returned would not suffer such friendships gladly, for Ireland was now heading for its inevitable crisis.

Ireland in Conflict A few months before the men of the 36th (Ulster) Division went 'over the top' at the Battle of the Somme, the Easter Rising had taken place in Dublin. While this insurrection was a failure — and resented by most Irish citizens, many of whom had sons, fathers or brothers dying unsung in France — the subsequent execution of its leaders finally swayed Irish opinion in favour of its instigators, and, as Yeats described it, "a terrible beauty" was born.

In 1918 Sinn Fein won a majority of Irish seats at Westminster, and the first self-styled Dáil Eireann (Government of Ireland) met in Dublin in 1919.

When this was declared illegal there followed a bloody War of Independence fought by the Irish Republican Army (IRA), the British forces being 'aided' by the notorious 'Black and Tans', whose activities merely alienated the population.

Lloyd George tried a compromise settlement in 1920, which provided for separate parliaments in Northern and Southern Ireland. Six counties in the north-east became Northern Ireland in 1921. The other twenty-six counties became the 'Irish Free State' in 1922 following an Anglo-Irish Treaty, but the Dominion status of the new State was not acceptable to Republicans. Civil War then erupted between pro- and anti- Treaty factions, the former led by Michael Collins, the latter by Eamon de Valera. During the last six months of this war, nearly twice as many Republican prisoners were executed by the authorities of the Free State as were executed by the British in the period from 1916 to 1921. It all ended with government victory in 1923.

In 1926 de Valera formed his Fianna Fail (Warriors of Destiny) Party. The Free State Party (Cumann na nGaedhael) lost power to Fianna Fail in 1933 and changed its name to Fine Gael (Tribe of Gaels) the following year. How many of either party were Gaels in either language, culture or ethnic origins is open to discussion. De Valera's basic Catholic nationalism was highlighted by a radio broadcast on St Patrick's Day, 1935 when he said "Since the coming of Saint Patrick... Ireland has been a Christian and a Catholic nation... She remains a Catholic nation." This statement demonstrates, according to Conor Cruise O'Brien, "the peculiar nature of Irish nationalism, as it is actually felt, not as it is rhetorically expressed. The nation is felt to be the Gaelic nation, Catholic by religion. Protestants are welcome to join this nation. If they do, they may or may not retain their religious profession, but they become as it were, Catholic by nationality." [93]

In 1937 de Valera was thus able to produce a new Constitution which was in essence a documentation of contemporary Roman Catholic social theory. Not unnaturally it had its attractions for the Catholics of Northern Ireland, especially since Craigavon, the first Prime Minister of Northern Ireland, who had "turned Ulster into a nation",[94] had announced three years previously: "all I boast is that we are a Protestant Parliament and a Protestant state". Yet from the outset Carson had pleaded that the Catholic minority should have nothing to fear from the Protestant majority: "Let us take care to win all that is best among those who have been opposed to us in the past. While maintaining intact our own religion let us give the same rights to the religion of our neighbours." That this reconciliation was not achieved was due to faults on both sides. It is a tragedy of Irish history that the men who now dominated Northern Ireland were far removed in their vision from those radical ancestors who in their own day had shown that the North could be the most enlightened part of the island. On both sides of the 'Partition' the political and religious establishments entrenched themselves behind ultra-conservative and rigid mentalities, and within Northern Ireland the two communities became beleaguered, each by the other.

Jack White   The intricate web that was now Irish politics — containing within it a profusion of conflicting religious, cultural, national and class loyalties — is perhaps best explored through the life-histories of individuals, rather than within the numerous academic textbooks on Irish politics. One prime example is the career of Jack White, whose story epitomises the complexity of Irish political life, a complexity which, while it may be readily understood by the Irish themselves, frequently bedevils 'outside' political commentators who try to analyse the Irish political psyche.

Gerard Burns has written: "The period leading up to the Easter Rising of 1916 produced many memorable characters, including the neglected Captain James Robert White, DSO, who virtually single-handedly forged the Irish Citizen Army into an effective fighting force. White himself did not take part in the uprising and this, probably more than anything else, has meant that today he is a largely forgotten figure. Nevertheless, he was for a time a central figure in a turbulent period which saw the rise of militant Irish labour, the demise of the Irish Parliamentary Party and its replacement by an aggressive Irish nationalism, and in the North, the development of intransigent Carsonite Unionism." [95]

Jack White was born in County Antrim, the son of Field Marshal Sir George White VC, who held almost every honour the British Army could bestow, especially after his defence of Ladysmith during the Boer War. The family were part of the Anglo-Irish landowning class, and Jack White followed his father into the Army. He was awarded the DSO after seeing action against the Boers at Magersfontein and Doorknop. An incident at the latter engagement gives a clear indication of his character. Advancing towards the enemy lines they found only one Boer left, a terrified teenage boy. One of White's fellow officers ordered the boy to be shot. "If you shoot him," retorted White, "I'll shoot you." White eventually dropped out of the Army and worked his way around Europe and North America.

When he returned to Ireland Sir Edward Carson was rallying the Protestants of the North in their resistance to the proposed Home Rule Bill. The leading barrister of his day, Carson's "magnificent presence and rock-like attachment to the cause provided perfect leadership." [94] Undeterred, White organised one of the first Protestant meetings, at Ballymoney, which opposed the Irish Unionist position, speaking on the platform alongside another prominent Protestant, Sir Roger Casement. Carson was too strong in the North, however, and White was invited to Dublin. There he met the Irish Socialist leader, James Connolly, and offered his services to the working-class cause during the time of the 'Dublin lock-out'. White addressed a mass meeting in Liberty Hall and proposed that a drilling scheme be started as a means of bringing discipline "into the distracted ranks of Labour". Samuel Levenson has commented: "Short-tempered, a commanding speaker, versed in military affairs, he gave lavishly of his knowledge, time and money to the Citizen Army when it was first formed. On the following evening, 13 November, the Civic League held its first meeting, and the formation of the Citizen Army was announced." [96]

White was to be wounded when an unemployed procession, led by himself and four other Citizen Army leaders, was charged by police. The confrontation shocked conservative Irish opinion, and, soon afterwards, when White offered to put a section of the Citizen Army at the disposal of the Irish Volunteers, the latter organisation replied that it could not enter into relations with a body that had recently been in conflict with the police.

Two incidents while White was in the North highlight the contradictory nature of Irish political attitudes. On one occasion Connolly had booked St Mary's Hall in Belfast to protest against the agitation for partition. When White addressed the mainly Catholic working-class audience he was given a vociferous reception and an attentive hearing by the capacity audience, while Connolly received a lukewarm reception. The chairman of the meeting, William McMullen, was of the opinion that White's enthusiastic reception was due to him having forsaken the traditional politics of his family and having come over to the nationalist side. However, when White went to Derry to organise a brigade of Irish Volunteers there and was dismayed by the sectarian attitudes some of them held, he was dismissed as just 'defending his own' when he tried to reason with them.

When the First World War broke out White joined an Australian ambulance unit, but his association with Casement — who was to be hanged for treason after he tried to obtain guns for the Irish Nationalist cause from the Germans — meant that here too he was constantly regarded with suspicion. His 'own' people in Ulster, the Anglo-Irish establishment, had long regarded him as a 'Shinner', so the cycle of suspicion was complete.

When Connolly was sentenced to be executed for his part in Dublin's Easter Rising, White took the one step he felt might save his friend — he rushed to South Wales and tried to bring the Welsh miners out on strike. For that he was sentenced to three months imprisonment.

With the outbreak of the Spanish Civil War, White, like many other Irishmen, went off to fight for the beleaguered Spanish Republic, though he soon expressed disagreement at the way he felt the Communists were manipulating the International Brigades. However, in Spain White was to witness a situation which convinced him that there was an alternative not only to the stagnant political attitudes of Ireland but to authoritarian Communism. As he recalled later to Albert Meltzer, he discovered, much to his surprise, that a profound social revolution was taking place within the areas controlled by the Spanish Republic.[97] This popular revolution, spearheaded by anarcho-syndicalists, was attempting to establish a totally new form of society. Factories were taken over by their workers; the countryside by the peasants; Barcelona — a city of one and a quarter million people — was being fed and controlled by its own citizens; and all of this organised in a vast co-operative effort which has been described as "the greatest experiment in worker's self-management that Western Europe has ever seen". [98]

White threw himself enthusiastically into this people's revolution, training Spanish militiamen and village women in Catalonia in the use of firearms, and speaking at meetings in London on behalf of the anarchist trade union, the CNT (Confederación Nacional del Trabajo). However, the gradual destruction of the revolution by an alliance of Republican and Communist political parties weakened the popular effort in the Civil War and Franco and his Fascist allies eventually overwhelmed the Republic. White returned to Ireland where he died in 1940.

The Second During the Second World War, though their country was neutral,
World War more than 80,000 Southern Irishmen fought with great valour under the British flag. There were also 38,000 volunteers from Northern Ireland and some 4,500 were killed. Ireland also produced some of the finest military captains of the War, most of them from Ulster. During 1940, when the United Kingdom stood alone against the might of Nazi Germany, Winston Churchill committed the leadership of the British Army to the great Ulster generals Sir John Dill, Alan Brooke, Claude Auchinleck, Bernard Montgomery and Harold Alexander, who proved to be among the best soldiers of all time.

In April and May, 1941, as the price of its loyalty to the Allied cause, Belfast suffered four air raids by German bombers. There was a heavy loss of life — almost 1,000 people perished — and 2,500 were injured, many of them seriously. In one particular raid no other city in the United Kingdom, save London, suffered such a high death toll.

In his victory broadcast of 13 May, 1945, Churchill affirmed that "if it had not been for the loyalty and friendship of Northern Ireland we should have been forced to come to close quarters or perish for ever from the earth." And while he deprecated the actions of the Dublin government in denying the Allies Irish ports and airfields, he was full of praise for the "temper and instinct of thousands of Southern Irishmen who hastened to the battle-front to prove their ancient valour." He could "only pray that the shame will be forgotten and the glories will endure, and that the peoples of the British Isles, as of the Commonwealth of Nations, will walk together in mutual comprehension and forgiveness."

The Republic Following the war, Southern Ireland left the British
Emerges Commonwealth and a 'Republic of Ireland' was formally constituted on Easter Monday 1949. However, emigration to England continued on a large scale, so that a sizeable proportion of its inhabitants are today of Irish descent.

The Republic of Ireland became known by the Gaelic name of 'Eire' (from the Old Gaelic 'Eriu'). Northern Ireland continued to be colloquially called 'Ulster', though Irish Nationalists disapproved of the six counties contained within the State being so labelled. Ironically, the Nationalists' nine-county

'Historic Ulster', was in reality an Elizabethan invention, and didn't correspond with the area traditionally accredited to Ulster in the ancient sagas, or the old tribal federation of Uladh (Ulidia) which consisted mainly of Antrim and Down, or even with the Gaelic Kingdom of the 14th to 16th centuries.

Southern Intransigence On both sides of the 'border' narrow political outlooks and uncompromising attitudes predominated, and inevitably intruded into the sphere of religion. The Protestants who remained in Eire after 1920 were soon to see a great reduction in their numbers. No one could be employed in any Civil Service unless she or he could speak Gaelic. Eire Governmental discriminatory measures included opposition to birth control and divorce and the banning of 'anti-Catholic' literature. 'Mixed-marriages' regulations which bordered on overt racialism were enforced by the Irish Roman Catholic Church. Dr Noël Browne's 'Mother and Child' scheme of 1951, proposing an element of State subsidisation of health care for pregnant mothers and their children, was opposed by the Irish Roman Catholic hierarchy. Browne was a member of the radical republican party Clann na Poblachta (Republican Family) whose leader, the ex-chief of staff of the IRA, Sean MacBride, called on him to resign. In the Parliamentary debate following Brown's resignation MacBride spoke for most in the Dáil when he said: "Those of us in the House, who are Catholics are, as such, bound to give obedience to the rulings of our church and our hierarchy." Such sentiments, allied with other forms of cultural and religious domination, were an important contributary factor in reducing the substantial Protestant population in the Republic of Ireland by at least one half. Indeed, on another defeat in the Eire Parliament, this time on his divorce bill, Noël Browne professed that he "would like to introduce a second motion, that the name of the State be changed to the Irish Holy Roman and Apostolic Republic."

Northern Entrenchment In Northern Ireland a similarily inward-looking and culturally defensive process had been well entrenched. From Northern Ireland's founding in 1921 a great sense of insecurity had enveloped the Unionist community, an insecurity highlighted by fears that a Boundary Commission would whittle away parts of the new state, and by the 'non-recognition' policies of Catholic political and civic leaders. These policies included a boycott of the new parliament at Stormont, and other practices such as Catholic teachers refusing their salaries from the Northern Ireland government and being paid direct from Dublin for almost a year. Even worse, an IRA campaign launched within the six counties heightened communal tensions and there was an outbreak of vicious sectarian violence in 1921 and 1922.

To counter all the real and perceived threats to its existence the Unionist administration initiated, encouraged or condoned discrimination in employment, education and housing, establishing in reality the anti-Catholic biases the minority assumed had always been there in principle. The strategy of Nationalist

100

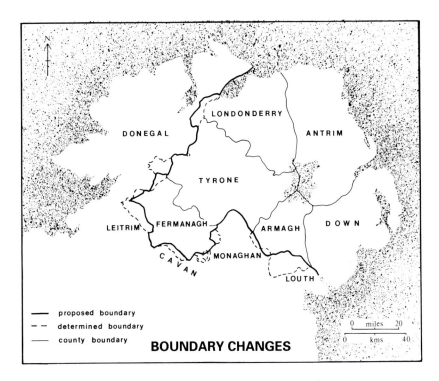

DONEGAL

LONDONDERRY

ANTRIM

TYRONE

LEITRIM

FERMANAGH

ARMAGH

DOWN

CAVAN

MONAGHAN

LOUTH

proposed boundary

— — determined boundary

county boundary

0   miles   20

0   kms   40

BOUNDARY CHANGES

and Unionist politicians alike served to convince much of the Catholic community that Northern Ireland was an 'Orange State', to which they could never belong.

A Narrow Gap   Yet whatever specific grievances Northern Ireland Catholics held towards the Stormont administration, such grievances still served to hide the underlying *reality* of the problem — that the narrow gap between the Catholic and Protestant working classes in Northern Ireland was much less significant than the gap between Northern Ireland and the rest of the United Kingdom, where on many indicators — such as housing conditions and unemployment — the citizens of Northern Ireland were much worse off.

Worries of Protestant working-class discontent also featured in 'Big House' Unionist thinking. As Richard Rose has observed, there had always been, because of their greater numbers, "more poor Protestants than poor Catholics" in Northern Ireland. The notorious discrimination against Catholics in both central and local government was not a device to further the material interests of Protestant working people but a political strategy which allowed the Unionist leadership to represent Catholics in general as a continuing threat to the Union, which only Protestant unity could fend off.

At the same time those who claimed to represent the socialist vanguard in Britain and Ireland remained trapped in nationalist ideologies.

Growing   The growing advantages of the British Welfare State and an
Posperity   improvement in the job mobility of the increasing Catholic
                population within Northern Ireland led to an ambivalent atitude towards the IRA. Indeed, the IRA leadership openly acknowledged the lack of popular support for the border campaign of 1956-62 in their cease-fire statement: "Foremost among the factors motivating this course of action has been the attitude of the general public whose minds have been deliberately distracted from the supreme issue facing the Irish people — the unity and freedom of Ireland."

The improved social and political climate in the early Sixties encouraged middle-class Catholics to press for an equal role within their society, and this seemed to be supported by the Northern Ireland Prime Minister Terence O'Neill, from a Unionist landed family of ancient Ulster lineage, who was considered to be more pragmatic than his predecessors, and sought to build bridges with the Catholic community.

However, O'Neill's approaches to the minority, tentative though they were, alarmed a significant section of the Unionist community, while the newly-emergent Catholic leadership, impatient with Unionist hesitation, took their grievances onto the streets through the Northern Ireland Civil Rights Movement. Unless Irish history was about to break with the patterns of the past, confrontation was now inevitable. Disturbances at a banned Civil Rights march through Londonderry on 5 October 1968 initiated the latest, and most tragic, period of the 'Troubles'.

When the militant student leader Bernadette Devlin was caught up in the confrontation during that 5 October march, her description of the violence, while graphic in its detail, is more revealing through her assessment of its significance, and as such highlights the deep sense of minority estrangement which had been festering below the surface: "Arms and legs were flying everywhere, but what horrified me was the evil delight the police were showing as they beat people down, then beat them again to prevent them from getting up, then trailed them up and threw them on for somebody else to give them a thrashing. It was as though they had been waiting to do it for fifty years." [99]

The Troubles   With the beginning of this new phase of conflict in Northern
                   Ireland many deep-seated fears were re-awakened within both communities. Each community's stereotyped image of the other now assumed reality porportions, and previously-held suspicions and doubts received apparent confirmation.

The catalogue of death and destruction which beset Northern Ireland over the next two decades has been extensively analysed by the world media and professional historians alike. As the communities plunged into a nightmare of

102

murder, revenge murder and relentless destruction, it seemed impossible that bridges could have been built. Yet among ordinary people, and through a variety of community groups, cross-community contacts were maintained in the face of all the violence, some of these attempts at community understanding containing more dialogue in one day's effort than had been undertaken by the various political parties over several months.

Yet even to those who strove to build something positive within the mayhem, the violence at times was of such an intensity that it repeatedly threatened to destroy any realistic hopes for dialogue and compromise. The violence perpetrated by all sides to the conflict bewildered the ordinary citizen, not just because of its unremitting nature, but because of the deep hatreds displayed by the combatants. After two elderly Protestants were gunned down by the IRA in 1988 for engaging in repair work to a police station, a local newspaper columnist wrote: "Someone said that Irish nationalism consists not of love of one's country but of hatred of someone else's. 'Their moving spirit,' he said, 'is not love of Ireland, but hatred of Britain.' If this is so, it may go some way towards explaining the frightfulness of the IRA onslaught on the citizens of this part of the island. The depth of the hatred they feel must be so intense as to suppress the normal instinct of revulsion which would restrain other people, however motivated, from firing 150 automatic bullets into two blameless and defenceless men as they made their way home after a hard day's work in County Fermanagh." [100]

The Facts of History If, indeed, it was the opposing interpretations of Irish history which lay behind the violence, or at least offered one of its main justifications, then much of the blame for preceding events must be laid squarely at the door of those who had used history for their own narrow ends, or those who had been strangely reticent in correcting the gross misinterpretations which had become so deeply entrenched in the popular imagination they seemed impossible to dislodge.

In the Republic, right from the foundation of the State, a Gaelic Nationalist myth was purveyed which sought to establish a solid pedigree for a Catholic/Celtic/Irish identity. Other contributions to this island's heritage were downgraded, if not completely ignored. Although it was obviously realised from the outset that such a self-image was fundamentally flawed, it seemed better to maintain silence rather than risk upsetting this newly-found identity. How else could one account for the fact that for 80 years after the foundation of the Gaelic League there did not exist a complete textbook of early Irish history?

In the South the time had come, as Bob Quinn suggested, when the Irish people "must develop the confidence to dismantle the unitary myth that has served its honourable purpose and replace it with the diverse richness that lies within." [101]

In Northern Ireland, a dislike of anything 'Irish', and a subservience to

103

'English' history within the schools, had left the Protestant community there not only unaware of most aspects of Irish history, but, more significantly, without any real understanding of the history of their own province. Yet Ulster's historical and cultural heritage was not only extremely rich and varied, but contained within it the proof of the common identity of the Northerners. Slowly, as contemporary flawed history was called into question and a new awareness emerged, the facts of their history, for once, rather than dividing them, offered the hope of uniting the Ulster people at last.

Chronology

6500 BC	Earliest evidence of man's presence in Ireland.
4000 BC	Neolithic Age sees the introduction of farming.
3350/2500 BC	Range of possible dates for the building of Newgrange passage-grave.
1800 BC	Working of bronze begins.
1200 BC	Making of gold artefacts.
600/500 BC	'Periplous', the Carthaginian, makes first documentary reference to Ireland.
330/300 BC	Greek geographer and traveller Pytheas makes earliest reference to the British Isles, calling them the 'Isles of the Pretani'.
200 BC	Use of iron in Ireland.
200/100 BC	Possible date for construction of Ulster's 'Great Wall'
100BC/100AD	First evidence of Celtic settlements.
100/200 AD	Period traditionally associated with the epic tales known as the 'Ulster Cycle', including the Cúchulainn saga.
130/180	Ptolemy the Greek provides the earliest known map of the British Isles.
431	The *Annals of Ulster* record the arrival of Palladius, sent by Rome to bring Christianity to Ireland.
432	The *Annals of Ulster* record the arrival of Saint Patrick.
444	Traditional date for Patrick's founding of Armagh.
445-53	Probable flourit of Niall Noígiallach, 'Niall of the Nine Hostages', from whom the greatest dynasty to emerge from among the Gaels, the Uí Néill, claim descent.
450	The Ulster capital at Emain Macha either falls to the Uí Néill or is abandoned by the Ulstermen as they retreat east of the Bann. Another massive earthen wall is erected to delimit part of the new, much-reduced boundary of Ulster.
475—516	The annals record numerous battles as the Uí Néill conquer the central plain of Ireland.
490	The Dál Riatai establish kingdom in Scotland.

545	*Annals of Ulster* record the founding of Derry by Columba (Colum Cille).
555	Cruthin abbot Comgall founds Bangor monastic settlement.
563	Cruthin suffer massive defeat at the hands of the Northern Uí Néill at the battle of Móin Dairi Lothair (Moneymore).
563	Iona founded by Columba.
579	Cruthin and Uí Néill clash near Coleraine.
589	Columbanus sets off on his great missionary journey to European mainland.
590	Columbanus' party establish their first church at Annegray in Burgundy. Second foundation later established at Luxeuil, followed by a third at Fontaine.
610—615	Columbanus expelled from Burgundy by local king. After a 600 mile journey he founds new monastery close to Lake Constance at Bregenz (in present-day Austria). Forced to vacate this location also, Columbanus founds his last monastic settlement at Bobbio in Northern Italy, where he dies in 615.
627	Congal Cláen of the Cruthin becomes over-king of Ulster.
637	Decisive Battle of Moira between Congal Cláen's Ulster forces and the Uí Néill leads to the Ulstermen's defeat and the end of any hopes they had of once again regaining control over the whole North. However, they still retain their independence in the east of Ulster for the next five hundred years.
735	The Ulaid suffer severe defeat at Fochairt near Dundalk at the hands of the Uí Néill.
750-800	Book of Kells illuminated. Flowering of Old Irish literature. Composition of Irish World Chronicle at Bangor.
795-837	Viking raids on Ireland, many monasteries sacked.
802	Iona raided by Vikings.
823	Norse pillage Bangor monastery.
827	Ulstermen fight alongside the Airgialla at the battle of Leth Cam but are defeated by the Uí Néill.
1169	The first 'Anglo-Normans' arrive on Irish soil, invited in by Dermot Mac Murchada, deposed King of Leinster.

1004	Battle fought at Cráeb Tulcha, in which many princes of Ulster are slain.
1177	John de Courcy marches north and captures Downpatrick. De Courcy styles himself 'Master of Ulster'.
1205	All de Courcy's land granted to Hugh de Lacy, who is created Earl of Ulster.
1314	In Scotland the English are defeated at the battle of Bannockburn by Robert the Bruce.
1315	Following the invitation by O'Neill of Tyrone to make Robert the Bruce's brother King of Ireland, Edward Bruce lands at Larne harbour.
1316	After a campaign of devastation Edward is crowned King of Ireland on 1 May, in the presence of a large assembly of Irish and Scottish nobles.
1318	Edward's forces finally defeated by John de Birmingham at Faughart near Dundalk. However the power of the Earls of Ulster is crushed. The O'Neills now begin to claim the whole of Ulster.
1364	For the first time the *Annals of Ulster* style an O'Neill as 'King of Ulster'.
1381	Niall Ua Néill attempts to legitimize his claim to Ulster at a great feast near Emain Macha. The term 'Ulster' now becomes used once again to cover the whole of the North.
1594	Following a new stage of the Engish conquest under Elizabeth I, a Gaelic rebellion is launched, led by the Northern clans, the O'Neills and O'Donnells. Hugh O'Donnell defeats an English army at the 'Ford of the Biscuits'.
1595	Sir Henry Bagenal and his English forces suffer heavy losses after ambush at Clontribret.
1598	O'Neill and O'Donnell dramatically defeat Bagenal at the Yellow Ford.
1601	The English under Mountjoy finally break the Gaelic rebellion at Kinsale.
1607	'Flight of the Earls', when many of Ulster's Gaelic chieftains sail from Rathmullan into voluntary exile. A new provincial configuration of Ireland has been effected by Elizabeth's

administrators, with Louth placed in Leinster and Breffny (Cavan) taken from Connaught and placed in Ulster.

1610	Ulster Plantation begins.
1641	Irish rebellion declared, with the rebels soon being supported by the Hiberno-English of the Pale.
1642	Owen Roe O'Neill returns to Ireland and forms his 'Catholic Army of Ulster'.
1646	The English forces defeated at Benburb by Owen Roe O'Neill and his forces, whom he terms 'the flower of Ulster'.
1649	Oliver Cromwell lands in Dublin, with Irish resistance already on the wane. He takes Drogheda by storm, then Wexford.
1652-3	Cromwellian land-confiscation against those who had participated in the rebellion.
1686	Richard Talbot is appointed by James II as Earl of Tyrconnell and General of the Forces in Ireland. He proceeds to dismiss all 'Englishmen' from the army and disband the Protestant regiments.
1688	Enniskillen and Derry defy James II. By the end of the year James is forced to abdicate the English throne.
1689	James' nephew and son-in-law, William, Prince of Orange and Nassau, is proclaimed King of England. James lands in Ireland and commences the Siege of Derry.
1690	William lands at Carrickfergus, and defeats James' forces at the Battle of the Boyne.
1691	James suffers futher defeat at Battle of Aughrim. The war ends with the surrender of Limerick.
1691-1791	Almost half a million of the defeated Jacobite soldiers, the 'Wild Geese', leave Ireland to form Irish Brigades of armies throughout Europe.
1695-1709	Penal leglislation against Catholics.
1704	Sacramental Test for public ofice, applicable both to Catholics and Protestant dissenters.
1717	Beginning of extensive migration of Ulster people to American colonies. By 1775 at least a quarter of a million had emigrated and become known as the 'Scotch-Irish'.

1737	Establishment of the *Belfast News Letter*, one of the world's first daily newspapers.
1771	Scotch-Irish settlers fight British forces on the Alamance River in North Carolina.
1775	Scotch-Irish settlers are the most prominent signatories of the Mecklenburg Declaration of Independence drawn up in Charlotte, North Carolina.
1776	Scotch-Irish support the Official Declaration of Independence passed by Continental Congress.
1782	Ulster Volunteer companies hold a convention at Dungannon, where they adopt resolutions favouring legislative independence and relaxation of penal laws.
1791	Founding of the Society of United Irishmen in Belfast by Presbyterian radicals.
1795	Sectarian clash at the 'Battle of the Diamond' in County Armagh leads to foundation of Orange Society, which later develops into the Orange Order.
1797	Government attempts to disarm the North. William Orr, one of the Presbyterian leaders of the United Irishmen, is hanged.
1798	United Irish rising in Leinster and Ulster. Henry Joy McCracken's United Army of Ulster takes Larne and Antrim but is defeated. Henry Munro's 'Hearts of Down' defeated at Ballynahinch. Both leaders executed.
1801	Following the failure of the rebellion Ireland is made part of the United Kingdom under an Act of Union.
1823	Daniel O'Connell forms the Catholic Association to press for Catholic Emancipation.
1845-49	The 'Great Famine' devastates Ireland; a million perish, and a further million emigrate, many to America.
1870	Home Rule movement launched in Dublin.
1886	Gladstone introduces Home Rule Bill in House of Commons.
1892	12,000 delegates at convention in Belfast oppose Home Rule.
1893	Gladstone introduces second Home Rule Bill, leading to disturbances in Belfast. Foundation of Gaelic League.
1905	Ulster Unionist Council formed. Sinn Fein founded.

1913	Ulster Volunteer Force, Irish Citizen Army and Irish Volunteers founded.
1914	First World War breaks out.
1916	Battle of the Somme, in which the 36th(Ulster) Division and the 16th(Irish) Division play a prominent role.
1916	'Easter Rising' in Dublin, followed by execution of its leaders.
1917	Battle of Messines, in which the 36th and 16th Divisions again play a prominent role.
1918	Sinn Fein win majority of Irish seats at Westminster, and set up Dáil Eireann.
1919—21	When Dáil Eireann is declared illegal, War of Independence is fought by the Irish Republican Army (I.R.A.).
1921	Separate parliaments set up North and South.

Sources

The Publishers acknowledge use of material from the following sources:

1   *The Mesolithic in Ireland*, Peter C. Woodman, British Archaeological Report 58, 1978.
2   Séan P. O Ríordáin, *Antiquities of the Irish Countryside*, Methuen, 1973.
3   W.C. Mackenzie, *The Races of Ireland and Scotland*, Alexander Gardner.
4   Michael Herity, *Irish Passage Graves*.
5   Colin Renfrew, *Before Civilisation*, Penguin 1983.
6   H.J. Fleure, 'Prehistoric elements in our heritage', *Bull. John Rylands Lib 18*, 1934.
7   P.A.O. Síocháin, *Ireland—A Journey into Lost Time*, Foilsiúcháin Eireann, Dublin.
8   Peter Woodman, 'Prehistoric Settlers', *The People of Ireland*, edited by Patrick Loughrey, Appletree Press/BBC, 1988.
9   Peter Harbinson, *Pre-Christian Ireland*, Thames & Hudson, 1988.
10 Estyn Evans, *The Personality of Ireland*, Blackstaff Press, Belfast, 1981.
11 John Kelleher, 'Early Irish history and pseudo history', *Studia Hibernica 3*, 1963.
12 W.G. Wood-Martin, *Traces of the Elder Faiths of Ireland*, Longmans, Green and Co., London, 1902.
13 Eamon de Buitléar, in an article by Gareth Huw Davies, *Radio Times*, 13-19 January, 1990.
14 Kevin Danaher, 'Irish folk tradition and the Celtic calendar', *The Celtic Consciousness*, Dolmen Press, 1981.
15 Estyn Evans, 'Ulster's First Farmers', *The Neolithic and Earlier Bronze Ages in the North of Ireland*, Humphrey Case and Arthur ApSimon, Institute of Irish Studies, Queen's University, Belfast, 1970.
16 E.G. Bowen, *Saints, Seaways and Settlements*, University of Wales Press, 1969.
17 J.P. Mallory, 'The Origins of the Irish', *The Journal of Irish Archaeology*, II, 1984.
18 Thomas L. Markey, 'The Language of Stonehenge', *L.S.A.*, University of Michigan, 1988.
19 F.J. Byrne, 'Early Irish Society', *The Course of Irish History*, The Mercier Press, 1984.
20 Eoin MacNeill, 'Where does Irish History Begin', *New Ireland Review 25*, March 1906.
21 Heinrich Wagner, 'Near Eastern and African connections with the Celtic World', *The Celtic Consciousness*, Dolmen Press, 1981.
22 David Greene, *The Irish Language*, Dublin, 1966.
23 Heinrich Wagner, *Studies in the origins of the Celts and of early Celtic civilisation*, Belfast-Tubingen, 1971.
24 Francis J. Byrne, *Irish Kings and High-Kings*, Batsford, 1973.
26 Chris Lynn, 'The Iron Gates of Ulster', *Pieces of the Past*, Department of the Environment for Northern Ireland, H.M.S.O., 1988.
25 Aidan Walsh, 'Excavating the Black Pig's Dyke', *Emania 3*, 1987.
27 Victor M. Buckley, 'From the Darkness to the Dawn', *The Borderlands*, Institute of Irish Studies, Queen's University, 1989.
28 *Silva Gadelica*, edited and translated by Standish Hayes O'Grady, Lemma Publishing Corporation, New York, 1970.
29 Douglas Hyde, *A Literary History of Ireland*, T. Fisher Unwin, London, 1906.
30 R.A.S. Macalister, *Ireland in Pre-Celtic Times*, Mannsell & Roberts, 1921.

31 *Táin Bó Cúalnge*, translated by Cecile O'Rahilly, Dublin Institute of Advanced Studies, 1970.
32 *The Táin*, Thomas Kinsella, Dolmen Press/Oxford University Press, Dublin, 1983.
33 Charles Doherty, 'Ulster before the Normans: ancient myth and early history', *Ulster—An Illustrated History*, Batsford, London, 1989.
34 A. H. Leahy, *Heroic Romances of Ireland*, Lemma Publishing Corporation, New York, 1974.
35 *Annals of Ulster*, edited, with a translation and notes, by William M. Hennessy, H.M.S.O., Dublin, 1887.
36 Tomás Cardinal O Fiaich, 'The Beginnings of Christianity', in *The Course of Irish History*, edited by T.W. Moody and F.X. Martin, The Mercier Press/RTE, Cork, 1984.
37 *A Dictionary of Irish Place-Names*, Adrian Room, Appletree Press, Belfast, 1986.
38 *Bangor—Light of the World*, Ian Adamson, Pretani Press, Belfast, 1979.
39 *The Illustrated Road Bok of Ireland*, The Automobile Association, 1970.
40 Proinsias Mac Cana, 'Mongán Mac Fiachna and *Immram Brain*', in *Eriu*, vol. XXIII, Dublin, 1972.
41 Adamnani, *Vita S. Columbae*, edited from Dr Reeves' text with an introduction by J.T. Fowler, Oxford, 1894.
42 J.T. Fowler, introduction to *Vita S. Columbae*, op. cit.
43 Tomás O Fiaich, *Columbanus*, Veritas Publications, 1974.
44 H. Zimmer (quoted in 43)
45 Ian Wood, 'The *Vita Columbani* and Merovingian Hagiography', *Peritia*, Volume 1, 1982.
46 John Romer, *Testament*, Michael O'Mara/Channel 4, 1988.
47 G.S.M. Walker, *Works of St Columbanus*, Dublin 1957.
48 Duncan Norton-Taylor, *The Celts*, Time-Life Books, 1976.
49 *The Battle of Moira*, Samuel Ferguson's *Congal*, edited by Ian Adamson, Pretani Press, Belfast, 1980.
50 *Bechbretha*, edited by Thomas Charles-Edwards and Fergus Kelly, Dublin Institute for Advanced Studies, 1983.
51 T.F. O'Rahilly, *Early Irish History and Mythology*, Dublin Institute for Advanced Studies, 1984.
52 Charles Thomas, *Britain and Ireland in Early Christian Times*, Thames and Hudson, London, 1971.
53 G. Chalmers, *Caledonia*, London, 1807.
54 Liam de Paor, 'Roots', *Irish Times*, 15 July, 1975.
55 Liam de Paor, 'The People of Ireland', *The People of Ireland*, edited by Patrick Loughrey, Appletree Press/BBC, Belfast, 1988.
56 A.T. Lucas, 'The plundering and burning of Churches in Ireland', in Rynne (ed.), *North Munster Studies*, Limerick, 1967.
57 Lewis Warren, 'The Normans', *The People of Ireland*, op. cit.
58 T.E. McNeill, 'Lordships and invasions: Ulster, 1177-1500', *Ulster—An Illustrated History*, edited by Ciaran Brady, Mary O'Dowd and Brian Walker, Batsford, London, 1989.
59 Robert Kee, *Ireland—A History*, Sphere Books, 1982.
60 Denis Kennedy, 'Foreword' to T.M. Healy, *The Great Fraud of Ulster*, Tralee, 1971.
61 Rev George Hill, *An Historical Account of the Plantation in Ulster at the Commencement of the Seventeenth Century 1608-1620*, Belfast, 1877.

62 P.L. Henry, *Ulster Dialects*, Ulster Folk Museum, 1964.

63 F.J. Bigger, 'From Uladh to Galloway and From Galloway to Uladh', *The Red Hand Magazine*, vol 1 no 3, November 1920.

64 M. Perceval-Maxwell, *The Scottish Migration to Ulster in the Reign of James I*, Routledge and Kegan Paul, 1973.

65 De Bruce R. Trotter, *Galloway Gossip*, Dumfries, 1901.

66 A.T.Q. Stewart, *The Narrow Ground— Patterns of Ulster History*, Pretani Press, 1986.

67 Brendan Adams, *The Hand is Red* by Biggs-Davison, Johnson, London, 1973.

68 Jerrold I. Casway. *Owen Roe O'Neill and the Struggle for Catholic Ireland*, University of Pennsylvania Press, 1984.

69 Anne Hutton (ed.), *The embassy in Ireland of Mgr G.B Rinuccini*, Dublin, 1873 (quoted in *Borderlands*, edited by Raymond Gillespie and Harold O'Sullivan, The Institute of Irish Studies, Queen's University of Belfast, 1989).

70 G.M. Trevelyan, *A Shortened History of England*, Penguin, 1974.

71 Lord Macauley, *The History of England from the Accession of James the Second*, Macmillan, 1913.

72 J.M. Barkley, *Francis Mackemie of Ramelton*, The Presbyterian Historical Society of Ireland, Belfast, 1981.

73 J.O. Thorne and T.C. Collocott, *Chambers Biographical Dictionary*, Cambridge, 1984.

74 W.K. Sullivan and Richard Bagnell, 'Ireland: History', *The Encyclopaedia Britannica*, Ninth Edition, Vol XIII, Adam and Charles Black, Edinburgh, 1880.

75 Raymond Gillespie and Harold O'Sullivan, in their 'Introduction' to *Borderlands*, The Institute of Irish Studies, The Queen's University of Belfast, 1989.

76 *America's Historylands*, National Geographic Society, Washington, D.C., 1962.

77 W.F. Marshall, *Ulster Sails West*, Genealogical Publishing Co., Inc., Baltimore, 1979.

78 Fred A. Shannon, *American Farmers' Movements*, Anvil Press, Princeton, N.J., 1957.

79 W.H.A. Williams, 'Irish Traditional Music in the United States', *America and Ireland: 1776-1976*, Greenwood Press, USA, 1980.

80 Harold R. Alexander, *The Mecklenburg Declaration of Independence*, Ulster Heritage, Glenolden, P.A., 1978.

81 James G. Leyburn, *The Scotch-Irish: A Social History*, Chapel Hill, The Univeristy of North Carolina Press, 1962.

82 Peter Smyth, introduction to *The Volunteers, 1778-84*, Educational Facsimiles 141-160, Public Records Office of Northern Ireland.

83 Thomas Pakenham, *The Year of Liberty*, Panther Books, London, 1972.

84 Mary McNeill, *The Life and Times of Mary Ann McCracken*, Allen Figgis & Co., Ltd., Dublin, 1960.

85 Rory Fitzpatrick, *God's Frontiersmen: The Scots-Irish Epic*, Weidenfeld and Nicolson/Channel 4/UTV, London, 1989.

86 R.R. Madden, *Antrim and Down in Ninety-Eight*, Cameron & Ferguson.

87 McGimpsey, Christopher, *Ulster Protestant Nationalism, c. 1690-1900*, West Belfast Historical Society, 1982.

88 Eoin MacNeill, 'The North Began', *An Claidheamh Soluis*, 1 November, 1913.

89 A.T.Q. Stewart, *The Ulster Crisis*, Faber and Faber, London, 1979.

90   Frank A. Mumby (Ed.), *The Great War—A History*, The Gresham Publishing Company.

91   H.E.D. Harris, *The Irish Regiments in the First World War*, The Mercier Press, 1968.

92   Brigadier A.E.C. Bredin, *A History of the Irish Soldier*, Century Books, 1987.

93   Conor Cruise O'Brien, *States of Ireland*, Hutchinson, 1972.

94   'The Ulster Crisis', Maurice Shock, in *History of the 20th Century*, Paulton, 1968

95   Gerard Burns, *Irish Times*, 15 September 1978.

96   Samuel Levenson, *James Connolly—A Biography*, Quartet Books, London, 1977.

97   Albert Meltzer, 'From Loyalism to Anarchism', introduction to *The Meaning of Anarchism*, J R White, Cienfuegos Press.

98   *The Spanish Civil War*, David Mitchell, Granada Publishing/Granada TV, 1982.

99   Bernadette Devlin, *The Price of my Soul*, Andre Deutsch, London, 1969.

100 Quoted in *20 Years: A Concise Chronology of Events in Northern Ireland, 1968-1988*, Island Publications, 1988.

101 Bob Quinn, *Atlantean*, Quartet Books, London, 1986.

Index

McCabe, Thomas, 84
McClelland, George B., 81
McCracken, Henry Joy, 84ff
McCracken, Mary Ann, 86
Megalithic burial monuments: building of, 3; continuing popular respect for, 4; use as royal sites by Celtic chiefs, 11
Megalithic inhabitants: at the core of our heritage, 3; as the primary ancestors of the Irish people, 4; at the roots of cultural personality, 4; Ireland as final stronghold, 8; evidence of continuity of tradition under Celtic overlay, 11
Mesolithic Age, 3
Messines, battle of, 95
Metallurgy, introduction of, 6
Mil, Sons of, 44
Mochaoi (Saint), 27
Móin Dairi Lothair, battle of, 38
Moira, battle of, 38ff
Moiry Pass, 16
Montgomery, Field Marshal, 99
Mountjoy, Lord, 70
Mount Slemish, and St Patrick, 27
Movilla, 28, 49
Mug Nuadat, 13
Muirthemne, 18, 20, 49, 59
Munro, Henry, 86

National Repeal Association, 89
Navan Fort (see Emain Macha)
Neilson, Samuel, 84, 87
Nendrum, 27
Neolithic Age, 3
Newgrange, 3
Niall Noígiallach, 'Niall of the Nine Hostages', 14
Ninian (Saint), 27
Non-Indo-European (see Pre-Celic)

North Channel: link during neolithic period, 3, 45; and Dál Riata, 46; 'culture province' during sixth and seventh centuries, 47
Northern Star, 84
Nugent, James Roland, 73

O'Brien, Charles, 73
O'Connell, Daniel, 88, 89, 90
O'Donnell, Balderg, 73
O'Donnells, 15, 52, 57
Ogham, 9
O'Higgins, Bernardo, 89
O'More, Rory, 63
O'Neill, Owen Roe, 64, 65
O'Neill, Sir Phelim, 63, 65
O'Neill, Terence, 102
O'Neills, 14, 15, 52, 53, 57
Orange County, Virginia, 75
Orange Society, 85
Orange Order, 85, 88
Ormonde, Lord Lieutenant, 68
Orr, William, 85

Paine, Thomas, 84
'Pale', the, 57, 59, 63
Palladius, 24
'Pangs of Ulster', the, 19
Parnell, Charles Stewart, 91
'Partition', 96
Patrick (Saint): arrival of, 24; life of, 27
'Patriot Parliament', 69
Penal Laws, 74
Pennsylvania Line, 77
'Pentland Rising', 66
'Periplous' of Himilco, 7
Picts: Pretanic origins, 8, 48; and kings of Dál Riata, 46; 'Picts of Galloway', 46; in make-up of medieval Scotland, 48; having language similarities with Irish Cruthin, 48

Tone, Theobald Wolfe, 84, 87
Travis, William Barrett, 80
Tuathal Techtmar, 13
'Twins of Macha', 17

Uí Echach Cobo, 42
Uí Néill: rise of, 14; embark on
    conquest of Ulster, 14; defeat
    Cruthin at battle of Móin Dairi
    Lothair, 38; defeat Ulstermen at
    battle of Moira, 39; and high-
    kingship, 40; defeat Ulaid at
    Fochairt, 41; defeat Airgialla at
    battle of Leth Cam, 41; defeat
    Ulstermen at Cráeb Tulcha, 41;
    establish their genealogical
    credentials, 44; confront first
    'Anglo-Normans', 51; claim the
    whole of the North after the
    destruction of the Earldom of
    Ulster, 53
Ulaid, the: as the *Voluntii* on
    Prolemy's map, 15; confront the
    Uí Néill, 15; defeated at
    Fochairt, 41; clash with the
    Vikings, 49
Ulster: in prehistoric period, 15; as
    depicted in the 'Ulster Cycle',
    16; as cradle of Christianity in
    Ireland, 27; as cradle of written
    Irish literature, 31; territory
    reduced after battle of Moira,
    41; encompasses the whole
    North again following
    extinction of kingdom of Ulaid,
    53; has its boundaries re-drawn

by Elizabethan administrators,
    59; six counties become
    Northern Ireland, 96
'Ulster Chronicle', 30
'Ulster Cycle', 16
Ulster Division (36th), 93, 94
Ulster Volunteer Force, 92
United Irishmen, Society of, 84ff
'Usnach, The Children of', story
    of, 21

Verdun, 93
Vikings, 49, 50
Volunteer Movement, 83
Voyage of Bran, 30

War, First World, 93
War, Second World, 99
Washington, George, 78
Waterford, 49, 50
Wellington, Duke of, 89
Wexford: founded by
    Scandinavians, 49; taken by
    Cromwell, 65
White, Jack, 97ff
Wicklow, 49
Wigton Martyrs, 68
'Wild Geese', 73
William, Duke of Normandy, 50
William of Orange, 69ff
Wounded Knee massacre, 77

Yeats, W.B., 92, 95
Yellow Ford, battle of, 57
'Young Ireland' movement, 89

Titles available from Pretani Press

Bangor, Light of the World   *Ian Adamson*
The Cruthin   *Ian Adamson*
The Identity of Ulster   *Ian Adamson*
The Ulster People   *Ian Adamson*
Morning in Belfast   *Denis Greig*
Churchill and the Irish Marshals   *Patrick Marrinan*
Bombs in Belfast—The Blitz 1941
The Great War 1914-1918
Ulster: The Hidden History   *Michael Hall*
Holy War in Belfast   *Andrew Boyd*
The Cavalier Duke   *J. C. Beckett*